CAN YOU DIG IT?

* Do you find yourself on all fours
  digging holes in a flowerbed every Saturday?

* On those beautiful sunny summer days,
  do find yourself praying for rain?

* Do you show strangers pictures of
  your prize-winning squash?

* Do you have nightmares of giant rabbits
  destroying your cabbage?

From the latest in garden garb to the greatest green thumb achievements ever, this hilarious volume is filled with outrageous illustrations, jokes, quizzes, trivia, and anecdotes, and is the ideal book for gardeners and those forced to endure them.

THE UNOFFICIAL
GARDENER'S HANDBOOK

SHELLEY GOLDBLOOM lives with her husband on ten acres in Onalaska, Wisconsin, where over the years she's raised aphids, zucchini, goats, dogs, cats, ducks, chickens, and kids. Shelley teaches creative writing to adults at Western Wisconsin Technical College and hosts and produces "Good Neighbors" for National Public Radio member station WLSU. She is the author of *Garden Smarts: A Bounty of Tips from America's Best Gardeners.*

THE UNOFFICIAL
GARDENER'S
HANDBOOK

by
Shelley Goldbloom

Illustrations by
Mark A. Abellera

A PLUME BOOK

PLUME
Published by the Penguin Group
Penguin Books USA Inc., 375 Hudson Street,
New York, New York 10014, U.S.A.
Penguin Books Ltd, 27 Wrights Lane,
London W8 5TZ, England
Penguin Books Australia Ltd, Ringwood,
Victoria, Australia
Penguin Books Canada Ltd, 10 Alcorn Avenue,
Toronto, Ontario, Canada M4V 3B2
Penguin Books (N.Z.) Ltd, 182–190 Wairau Road,
Auckland 10, New Zealand

Penguin Books Ltd, Registered Offices:
Harmondsworth, Middlesex, England

First published by Plume,
an imprint of New American Library,
a division of Penguin Books USA Inc.

First Printing, March, 1992
10 9 8 7 6 5 4 3 2 1

 REGISTERED TRADEMARK—MARCA REGISTRADA

Library of Congress Cataloging-in-Publication Data:
Goldbloom, Shelley.
    The unofficial gardener's handbook / Shelley Goldbloom ;
illustrations by Mark A. Abellera.
      p.   cm.
    ISBN 0-452-26769-2
    1. Gardening—Humor. 2. Gardeners—Humor. I. Title.
PN6231.G3G65 1992
818'.5402—dc20   91-25211
                                                    CIP

PRINTED IN THE UNITED STATES OF AMERICA
Set in Clearface and Caxton Book

This book is dedicated,
with love,
to my mother, Beatrice Marjorie Kaplan Sperling,
who raised me according to her own
"Unofficial Guide to Everything in Life":
a sense of humor.

ACKNOWLEDGMENTS

My editor, Alexia Dorszynski, Elizabeth Pomada and Michael Larsen, my agents, and especially my daughter, Stefanie Eve Goldbloom, were my source for a whole bumper crop of ideas, and I owe them a debt of thanks.

Helen Mayville and Kate Frederick have my loving gratitude for their hand-holding, encouragement, and enthusiasm. Thanks also to Officer Paul Bequette of the La Cross Police Department for showing me how to write up arrest reports.

I also want to express my appreciation to zucchini grower extraordinaire Donna Fuss, horticulturists Jim Cook and Jean Williams, Anne Goldbloom, Fred Gray of the University of Wyoming School of Agriculture, Bea Sperling, Phil Ostrem, Kelly Hass, Betty Holey, Joyce Beilke, Meredith Hougen, Lila Neuhaus, Martha Schams, Eve Simon, and Sue Skifton for sharing ideas and true-life anecdotes.

Contents

It's hard to believe anyone would actually take the advice that appears on these pages seriously, but stranger things have happened. Therefore, I hereby warn you that all advice contained in this book is meant to be humorous: please don't eat the daisies or do anything else that you may be tempted to try after reading my book, because it's not gonna work, and I can't afford to have you sue me.

—*Shelley Goldbloom*

CHAPTER 1

Know Thyself

Are You a Natural-Born Gardener?

Are you a natural-born gardener? Find out with DIGGER (Diverse Inquisition into Grandiose Garden Endeavor Resources), a scientific screening test developed by the Association for the Diagnosis and Treatment of Obsessive, Addictive Soil Builders, Composters, and Transplanters.

If you can figure out the correct answers to enough of the questions that follow, then you fit the

profile of the natural-born gardener
and this book is for you. What if
you aspire to a green thumb but
fail the test? Don't despair! Simply
study this volume, then follow up
with a supplemental reading of
*Remedial Gardening: Hope for the
Perplexed.*

1. OBSESSION
(a) A 1976 movie starring Cliff Robertson and Genevieve Bujold,
directed by Brian DePalma.
(b) An affliction striking 78% of American households, especially
between March and September, resulting in dirty fingernails, sore
backs, and incurable optimism.
(c) Fragrance by Calvin Klein that comes in an oval bottle and smells
like vanilla but costs ten times as much (and you can't even use
it in cookies).

2. DIG
(a) A quaint slang term popularized in the 1960s by "hip" characters,
meaning *to feel great enthusiasm for* or *to understand.*
(b) Labor gardeners must undertake to prepare the soil; plant new
shrubs, vegetables, and flowers; remove dead shrubs, vegetables,
and flowers.
(c) A site whose purpose is to advance scientific and historical knowledge—or so archaeologists say, because they're embarrassed to
confess their fantasies of discovering ancient artifacts encrusted
with rubies and gold.

3. GREAT DIRT
(a) An abbreviation for *Great Dirt Plains,* the geographical designa-
tion for the West Central region of the United States, sometimes
known as America's breadbasket.
(b) Soil that yields better roses.
(c) The knowledge that your boss is having an affair with your next-
door neighbor.

4. AWFUL DIRT
(a) Hey, Mom will wash your mouth out with soap if you talk like
that!
(b) Soil fit only for layering in compost heaps.
(c) The knowledge that your spouse is having an affair with your
next-door neighbor.

5. GONE WITH THE WIND
(a) The most popular American novel ever written.
(b) Your bean poles an hour after you stake them.
(c) What occurs when someone at the table polishes off the last of the chili.

6. REALLY SHOVEL IT ON THICK
(a) What political candidates do throughout the campaign season.
(b) What gardeners do with manure just prior to the growing season.
(c) What a high school sophomore hoping to pass for a senior does with eye makeup.

7. LIKE A VIRGIN
(a) A nonspecific term used by Italian Renaissance art specialists attempting to establish authenticity of newly discovered painting.
(b) Land never before cultivated.
(c) Very early Madonna.

8. TINY TIM
(a) A notorious short, vicious gunman of Wild-West fame.
(b) A variety of miniature, allegedly prolific, but really vastly overrated, tomato.
(c) The pathetic, impoverished, crippled child in a sentimental Dickens story performed every Christmas by every amateur theatrical troupe in the English-speaking world.

9. CONTAINER
(a) Geopolitical military policy for the prevention of naked aggression in countries we presently don't get along with.
(b) Plastic and clay pots that serve as a more affordable version of fields for urban dwellers.
(c) Packaging designed by creative art director after market research determines which colors and graphics and layout will give people the urge to buy.

10. Finish this sentence: When you hear the word *cult*, which of the following comes to mind?
(a) *Cultured* people who go to opera, read magazines with no pictures, and liberally sprinkle their conversation with names of depressed Swedish philosophers.

(b) *Cultivating* your garden regularly, which will keep down weeds, fluff up the soil, prevent moisture from evaporating too quickly, and give you more glorious *cultivars*.
(c) A group of people with bizarre religious practices not in keeping with one's own.

11. CAT DANCING
(a) Tragic love story made into a movie starring Burt Reynolds.
(b) Feline activity performed in newly sown pea patch.
(c) Erotic art form banned in Cincinnati.

SCORING
How did you do?

If your answers were mostly *a*, you have an unfair advantage over the rest of us because you majored in American Studies at a top eastern school, landed a job in the research department for *Reader's Digest*, and always win at Trivial Pursuit. You may like having your feet in the soil, but you're really happiest when you garden with your brain.

If your answers were mainly *b*, you still have thirty-five quarts of tomatoes from last summer in your cellar and *all* the back issues of *Horticulture* magazine. Be glad this isn't a practical guide, because you already know everything you need to know about gardening.

If you answered *c* to the majority of questions, you're obviously in advertising and buying this for your mother, because you yourself would never consider tomato growing a way to "do lunch." But since you're skilled at recognizing a good buy when you see one, you'll also want to buy copies of this book for your brother-in-law, your best friend, your therapist, and your broker.

What Kind of Gardener Are You?

Are You a CPA-style Gardener? (CPA = Compulsive, Precise, Administrative)

CPAs view nature's whims as loopholes that must be closed. Like reliable accountants, such gardeners leave nothing to chance. To a CPA, the only good garden is a properly itemized garden, with every row organized according to schedule. If you exhibit the following characteristics you belong in this category:

* Wear a green eyeshade when gardening. Carry cultivator next to calculator in breast pocket.

* Maintain an extensive horticulture library. Keep all back

issues of garden magazines color-coded and in chronological order.

* Plant only according to meticulously drawn blueprints.

* Practice systematic crop rotation cycles. Never forget what went where the previous year. (See next item.)

* Keep an executive organizer to record the quantity of each variety planted, location, planting date, time to maturity, and expected yield.

* Always know exactly where the executive organizer is located.

* Plant only in perfectly aligned rows. Space every seed equidistant from its neighbor. Measure with ruler to ensure accuracy.

* Remain ever vigilant against infiltrating weeds. Cultivate continuously and take pride in keeping the soil between plants absolutely level, smooth, and bare.

* Prune every shrub to identical height and clip hedges with the aid of a carpenter's level.

* Fertilize on a strict schedule, noting dates on appointment calendar. Spray with a systemic fertilizer-insecticide-herbicide.

* Always clean, hone, oil, and return your tools to storage after each use.

* Disapprove of the "natural look" in gardens; your favorite type of plant is bonsai.

Are You a Child-of-Nature-style Gardener?

Folks who do the following will be your kindred spirits:

* Belong to organic growing cooperatives that sponsor sister cooperatives for political fugitives in the mountains of El Salvador.

* Want to be in touch with the earth, and so garden barefoot. For same reason, they eschew gloves and favor bare hands.

* Buy garden supplies from mail-order houses with photographs of bearded people and ethereal nature poetry in their catalogs.

* Own very few tools and borrow tools from neighbors when needed.

* Plant, prune, and harvest by phases of the moon.

* Shun new hybrid seeds; would never consider planting "All-America Winners." Gather and save own seeds to sow the following year.

* Sow extra rows of lettuce so the rabbits won't go hungry.

* Collect ladybugs for predator

control. Use grapefruit rinds for trapping garden snails.

* Prefer to nourish garden with dead fish. Second-choice fertilizer is barnyard manure.

* Believe pruning is unnatural. Think trees should express themselves, assuming any shape at will.

* Tolerate dandelions. Roast the roots for brewing, stir-fry the greens with brown rice, and bottle the flowers for winter wine.

* Talk to plants, preferably about philosophical matters.

* Are morally opposed to thinning garden rows. When task is unavoidable, they feel too guilty to pluck out the weakest seedlings; prefer to discard the strongest ones.

Are You a Yuppie-style Gardener?

If so, you'll recognize yourself in the following profile:

* Belong to support group for gardeners. Note: This is *not*

like your mother's garden club, where housewives met in a member's living room to drink coffee and share geranium clippings. Your group meets in a member's corporate boardroom and sends out for cappuccino. Members network and compare strategies for helping their gardeners elude U.S. immigration authorities.

* Consider a cellular phone essential garden equipment.

* Go to England to shop personally for garden implements. And you wouldn't dream of cleaning them; when they get dirty, you discard them and buy new ones.

* Learn all the latest methods of gardening (such as noveau French intensive gardening) via video, but subscribe to *Horticulture* and *Fine Gardening* for the advertising.

* Don goatskin gloves, French canvas pants, and matching jewel-toned clogs for turning on the sprinkler system.

* Utilize time-management skills learned at the office. You opt for quick-germinating, quick-growing varieties.

* Prefer herbs that most people don't know how to pronounce; you use them for seasoning gazpacho and making wine vinegar.

* Would never consider canning surplus tomatoes like grandma did. Instead, you sun-dry them to garnish pasta salad.

* Select as your fertilizer of choice imported bat guano, but in a pinch you'll settle for kelp.

* Forbid anyone to touch your plants—after all, if hand lotion can cause condoms to disintegrate, what might it do to the cellular structure of leaves?

* Believe that plants thrive in the presence of music, so you treat them to CD recordings of the orchestra of St. Martin's-in-the-Field performing Bach.

CHAPTER 2

Garden Lingo

Understanding Garden Talk: Gardener's Glossary

APHID
The insect world's version of the Holstein. Small sticky creatures that congregate in vast colonies on roses and other prize garden plants, sucking sap and in turn getting "milked" by ants. Ridding your ornamentals of these unprofitable beasts disrupts the ants' age-old economic system, like a scaled-down version of the government whole-herd dairy buyout.

ARCTIC, AVID
As with the Deadheads who happily drive two thousand miles to see a Grateful Dead concert, there's no limit to the lengths that dedicated AVID ARCTIC gardeners will go to see a tomato succeed. They are grateful at the appearance of the smallest nubbin of fruit— though more often than not before any ripen, the plant dies.

BEETS
Red root vegetable grown in vast quantities to supply every hospital patient in the nation with at least one meal daily. Best grown in childless households, as gardeners with children should expect to invest not only labor in growing beets, but also energy in nagging all comers to eat them.

BONSAI
Anorexic tree with distorted body image. With the help of a co-dependent gardener, at full maturity goes to incredible lengths to maintain the size of a seedling.

BROCCOLI
Vegetable that hosts tiny green worms, which are invisible until steamed, buttered, and plunked on your dinner guest's platter.

CATALOG
Propaganda literature that comes through the mail. Intended to brainwash readers with extravagant claims and seductive photographs with the aim of depriving them of self-control and good judgment.

COGNOSCENTI

Gardeners who are really in the know and want you to know it, too. When everyone else at the party is scheming to get that sexy dame/hunk alone in a corner, *they're* holding forth about soil inoculant, slug bait, and damping-off disease.

CULTIVAR

Cultivars start out as the figment of somebody's imagination and end up with fanciful names like those planned communities in Arizona. The term itself is satisfying to throw around because most gardeners (except COGNOSCENTI, see preceding entry) aren't quite sure *what* it means.

GROWING CONCERN
Either the name of a gardening store with a quick-witted proprietor, or the sinking feeling you get when not a single one of the seeds you planted four weeks ago has started to emerge yet.

FLOWERPOTS
Containers whose powers of attraction rival cat litter pans. Available in two primary varieties. (1) Sensitive to human and pet vibrations. At the slightest movement, this variety responds by promptly toppling over. (2) Sturdy and resistant to ambulation. Such flowerpots maintain stability by inflicting a backache on anyone attempting to relocate them.

GARDENING
See LEGALIZED GAMBLING.

HEALTH FOOD CROPS
The majority produce gritty little seeds that catch in your teeth. If you're lucky, you can grow varieties that taste like cardboard instead of brussels sprouts—but never like Doritos or Twinkies.

HOE
Tool inspired by Wrong-Way Corrigan, apt to end up far from the desired destination. When aimed at what you *thought* was a weed, it always lands on a flower instead.

HOSE
Long, thin water-carrying tube, generally made of vinyl, with invisible inbuilt target. Scientists have yet to explain the miraculous sonar capability of hoses, especially expensive, newly purchased ones with five-year warranties, to signal lawn mowers, guiding them to home in and cut the hose in half.

HOUSEPLANT
Vegetation that may live a whole lifetime—indeed, generations—in captivity. Lulled by the life of a pampered prisoner, the houseplant grows slavishly dependent upon its keeper and loses the ability to survive if set free.

HYBRID
Marriage aimed at producing offspring with the best qualities of each parent. Whereas in human couplings you're stuck with Junior whether or not he inherits the desired combination of looks and brains, with plants it's possible to toss out the failures. (See THROWBACKS.)

INDOOR IRRIGATION
Indoor gardeners may rest assured that even modern aides to houseplant watering, such as ultra-lite watering cans with ergonomically designed spigots and plastic tubing that connects to the sink, still maintain comfortably familiar routines, permitting rapid flowage through the drainage holes, over the furniture, down the wall, and onto the floor. Nor do modern methods threaten the ability of

potting medium to float from the top of the container onto supporting structures.

INSECTS
Sturdy, fertile, easily pleased little animals with remarkable powers to feast, thrive, and multiply even in habitats under constant attack from frenzied gardeners.

LEGALIZED GAMBLING
See GARDENING.

MOISTURE METER
Clever gadget that probes the soil of potted plants and tells you when they're thirsty. It does not, however, inform you when their roots have been injured by being stabbed with a sharp stainless-steel probe.

NEIGHBOR
The person whose roses never die over winter, whose grass stays flawlessly manicured, whose seedlings never fall victim to cutworm—and whose corn, flattened to the ground by the hailstorm that miraculously spared yours, causes secret gloating in your heart.

OPTIMIST
Gardener who plants all the expensive pony packs of bedding plants at the same time.

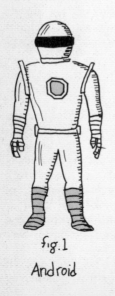

fig.1
Android

fig.2
Humanoid

fig.3
Plantoid

PESSIMIST
Gardener who buys a second set of pony packs to hold in the garage just in case the first batch fails.

PLANTOID
Any newly invented plant devised by anyone with profit in mind. Note: Many folks watching television coverage of the War in the Gulf were puzzled by CNN's frequent insertion of "FACTOIDS." Well, consulting linguists suggested that a "FACTOID" might be a factlike entity, the same way that a science fiction robot out to destroy the world may be called an ANDROID (from the male hormone, androgen, presumably) and creatures from other planets that look like us despite pointy heads and evil intentions are HUMANOIDS.

POTATO
Tuberous vegetable with an unmistakable, remarkably predictable sign of maturity: potatoes are ready to harvest once the top of the plant dies down so that you can no longer find it.

REALIST
Gardener who buys three sets of pony packs in order to have some on hand after the first two plantings fail.

RHUBARB
Nearly indestructible plant, hardy enough to grow through cement, argued to be edible.

ROTOTILLER
Gasoline-powered home plowing aide that is easier to maintain than a mule but a great deal more labor than a spade-wielding spouse. Costs (excluding fuel and repairs) the equivalent of forty years of paying the guy with the "Rototilling" ad in the paper.

SPADE
Sharp-edged tool akin to the Patriot missile, able to unerringly zero in on potatoes and other root vegetables and accomplish their destruction by slicing them sight unseen.

THROWBACK
Like the snaggly-toothed, sticky-outy-eared, big-nosed kid produced by seemingly perfect parents, THROWBACKS are offspring of gorgeous, prolific hybrids possessing weak and ugly attributes you never *dreamed* lurked in the ancestral gene pool. (Not to be mistaken for SPITBACK, the jellybean flavors eaten only as a last resort.)

TOPIARY
For the person with far-reaching interests, this art form transforms ordinary hedges into decoy ducks, allowing you to enjoy the pleasures of gardening, sculpting, antique collecting, and hunting all at once. Those whose tastes veer toward Disneyland memorablia can investigate the ever-popular

Mickey-Mouse style of hedge trimming.

VOLUNTEERS
Volunteer plants are those thousand points of light that provide beauty and sustenance on their own initiative. Like enthusiastic houseguests, some volunteers reappear long after the gardener bade them good-bye and may even be self-sowing and treat you to their offspring. Others, such as the sliver of potato peel that sprouts among the petunias, per-

severe and thrive under conditions of neglect.

WEED
Vigorous prolific plant that needs no care, is never subject to crop failure, and grows virtually anywhere.

ZUCCHINI
When filling the backseat of the average station wagon to capacity, the emblem of a confirmed gardener.

CHAPTER 3

What Every Smart Gardener Should Know

Tasks That Are and Are Not Officially Gardening

* If you stop pulling weeds long enough to snap open the beer brought to you by a member of your household, and drink it leaning against the fence, you're unquestionably still gardening.

* If you take a quick break and go indoors to grab a cold beer and drink it in the kitchen, with hands still covered by dirt, you're officially still gardening.

* If you take a break and go indoors just to use the bathroom, and wash your hands for that reason, and *then* while you're inside anyway linger long enough to gulp down a quick beer, it's technically still gardening.

* If you stroll over to your neighbors' yard directly from your garden without stopping to change your clothes, and you sit outside on their back steps still wearing muddy boots and share a couple of beers, you're *still* gardening—provided your neighbor is also taking a break from gardening and that you gripe almost as long about cabbage worms as you gossip about whose kid just got arrested.

* You still are officially gardening if in any of the above four situations you substitute non-diet carbonated beverages or homemade lemonade for beer. If you drink mineral water or iced tea, however, you've crossed over the line into the realm of "loafing."

27

* If your neighbor wanders over to your yard and you don't leave your position between the rows, then conversation on local politics, scandals concerning people within a twenty-mile radius, sex, or philosophy is still legitimate gardening, providing you keep a garden tool in hand. (Note: This situation ceases to be legitimate gardening if mutual funds, IRAs, national elections, or the war between the sexes is even mentioned.)

* Driving in your car anywhere within a ten-mile radius to borrow or retrieve a garden tool may be considered a valid gar-

dening chore. If you drive a truck you may increase the distance to a twenty-five-mile radius.

* One polite cup of coffee at your destination is within the realm of gardening. Staying for dinner is no longer gardening time. And drinking beer is out of the question—you shouldn't be drinking and driving.

* According to U.S. Census Bureau labor statistics, all moments spent reading the blurbs in garden catalogs when there's snow on the ground, flipping through gorgeous glossy photographs in gardening magazines, standing in other people's gardens while enviously (or scornfully) comparing them to your own, reading recipes with fruit or vegetable ingredients, trying on jeans in shopping malls, and daydreaming are computed into the Gross National Tally of Official Gardening Time.

Catalog Terms Translated

It's to your advantage, both in terms of time and money, to restrain yourself and not buy plants you're not going to be satisfied with. Unfortunately, it's often hard to know; garden catalogs are a lot like books touting various breeds of dogs—they never couch anything in negative terms. If you've ever shopped for a dog, you know what this means: the hyperactive, flighty piece of fluff is described as "alert," and when they call a brute "protective," you can be sure that if you get up at night to go to the bathroom, he'll mistake you for a burglar and take your leg off.

Fortunately, if you buy plants that don't satisfy you, you needn't bother with "GOOD HOME WANTED" ads in the classified section of your local newspaper. You can simply rip the plants out and fling them aside without worrying that your neighbor will report you to the Humane Society. On the other hand, you're not likely to splurge and buy twelve dozen poodles, but people have been known to buy more than twelve dozen tulip bulbs (and with dogs, you don't have to go through all that work of planting them).

So if you are considering purchasing those lavish offerings from catalogs, you'd be wise to learn to read between the lines by studying the following translations:

DELICATE BLOOMS
Flowers that die if you so much as look at them.

GRACEFUL STALKS
Plants that flop over in a wind.

FLOWERING PHASE
This is an optimistic figure that usually works out to be 2 days out of 365.

EARLY BLOOMING
This means your darlings will be hidden under the snow.

LATE BLOOMING
Frost will strike before the buds open.

LIKE RICH SOIL
Normal dirt will kill this plant; be prepared to become its slave.

NATURAL
This wonder looks just like the weeds.

WITH A LITTLE BIT OF EFFORT
This monster needs seasonal mulching, monthly pruning, weekly fertilizing, daily watering—and even then it probably won't survive.

PROLIFIC
You didn't need to buy this specimen, because it's growing wild all around you.

ROBUST
This one will invade your lawn so aggressively that your grass will be invisible in a month.

VIGOROUS
You'll never get rid of it.

CHAPTER 4

Getting a Grip on Basics

The Lowdown on Soil: It's a Dirty Business but Someone's Gotta Handle It

"TALK DIRTY TO ME"

A GARDENER'S GUIDE TO SOIL.

Get gardeners going about soil and their eyes will soon glaze over, giving them an expression on their faces like the one you see in the Renaissance paintings of the Apostle Paul on the Road to Damascus. Gardeners will gush on and on about the indefinable scent, the magical properties, the rich, life-sustaining power, until you begin to wonder if maybe you misunderstood and it's not soil they're talking about but peyote or uranium.

But in a candid moment, even the most fanatic soil lover will admit that dealing with garden dirt is actually one of the most troublesome aspects of gardening. Let's face it: dirt is—well, dirty. And it's heavy. Anyone who lives

in a third-floor walkup and needs to haul dirt up flights of steep, rickety stairs will scoff at the idea that dirt is mystical.

Dirt also has a habit of getting tracked all over the place and into everything. But, diabolically, even though it invariably gets places you *don't* want it, dirt doesn't automatically appear where you *do* want it. Not only urban folks, but even country gardeners often are at a loss to locate sources of top-quality dirt nearby. The following suggestions for getting

31

"good dirt" will put you on solid ground:

* Dirt's ubiquitous quality isn't *always* bad news. Stop nagging your family to wipe their feet when they come in, and let them track dirt to where you can readily collect it.

* For a long time now we've had artificial plants that look so real you have to stick your fingernail into a leaf to figure out whether it's genuine or not. New on the market is fake dirt. If you're a frugal gardener, Cheap Plastic Dirt is for you: granted, it looks really fake and is not going to fool anybody, but it costs little, lasts a long time, and is impervious to rain and snow. For a more upscale effect, there's Expensive Silk Dirt; yes, you'll pay a little more—but it's impossible to tell it from the real thing.

* Do-it-yourselfers can also make a homemade dirt from polyurethane foam packaging popcorn. Spray those babies with brown paint for more authenticity. And for a *really* authentic touch, add a sprinkling of bird lime, available free from most pet stores, and some worms from a bait shop.

* Sponsor an award at your neighborhood high school science fair for the student who can invent a clean, light, cheap dirt substitute.

* There are mind-control sects that claim thoughts have the power to cure disease, bring material wealth, and even get you a parking space. If this is so, then take a cue from all the skiers' bumper stickers exhorting "THINK SNOW"— "THINK DIRT." And if at first you don't succeed, try dirtier thoughts.

* Urban gardeners don't have to just sit around waiting for dirt to drift in from outer space; settling soot from the atmosphere is plenty dirty, and you'll get points from the neighborhood environmental team for recycling.

* For the ultimate form of dirt, shred *National Enquirers*.

Mulch Mystique

If you're smart, you'd never dream of risking a mulchless garden. After all, mulch keeps your garden safe: it helps prevent disease, it stops moisture from seeping out, protects against unwanted growth. It's a shield, in other words—something like a condom for your garden.

It's amazing, really. If you leave old newspapers, tar-paper scraps, hunks of carpeting, sheets of plastic, rocks, weeds, straw, or rotting kitchen scraps strewn around your yard, people call you a terrible slob. But pile up any or all of this debris between your garden rows, and what you've done is "mulching."

Even so, some gardeners worry that neighbors won't realize the stuff strewn around is not slobhood but wise husbandry, and so they resort to high-tech alternatives, such as mulches made from breathable plastics and spun nonwoven polyester.

Fashion-conscious gardeners, though, wouldn't be caught dead with anything as tacky as *synthetic* mulch. They understand that the mulch you use proclaims your taste just as do the magazines you read and the way you wear your hair. So to test your gardening acumen and hone your mulching skills, match the various mulching materials that follow with the garden personality that best describes *you:*

You use:
1. Back issues of *National Geographic.*
2. Reflective Mylar that mirrors back one's own image.
3. Mulches with vibrant Day-Glo sunburst designs.
4. Sequinned and beaded mulches.
5. Softly shirred silk for summer mulching; pleated 100-percent pure wool for winter mulching.
6. Canvas mulches hand-screened with authentic-looking replicas of Claude Monet's garden at Giverny (not the water-lily garden that's now such a cliché, but his *vegetable* garden, known only to a few art critics).
7. Macho mulch: black leather studded with silver metal rivets.
8. Dollar bills.
9. Invisible mulches spun from the same cloth used for the emperor's new clothes.

This means:
(a) You got an A+ in Art Appreciation 101.
(b) You know your garden would be even closer to perfection if you could figure out a way to add monogramming.
(c) You're trying to pull a few weeds between appointments and worry you'll mess your hair.
(d) You generally concentrate on cultural attractions like museums and famous monuments, but Hong Kong was a shopper's paradise.
(e) You want your plants to realize that you are the kind of person who donates to the Audubon Society, Sierra Club, and Nature Conservancy, and takes your environmental responsibilities seriously.
(f) Your favorite plants are ones with thorns—or daisies for making chains.

(g) You've never had use for the likes of that troublemaker Ralph Nader.
(h) You want your plants to be productive and believe it's important to provide them with suitable role models.
(i) California *is* the nation's garden center, as well as the cutting-edge of fashion, isn't it? You trust it!
Key: 1-e; 2-c; 3-i; 4-d; 5-b; 6-a; 7-f; 8-h; 9-g.
How did you do?

* Bravo if 1 is your answer! *You're* not going to sit idly by while people who refuse to throw away their old *National Geographics* are making the earth grow so heavy, it's sinking at a rate of three inches a year.
* If your personal mulch of choice is 2, 3, 4, or 5, then there's no doubt that not only your garden, but *you*, are absolutely gorgeous, though behind your back cattier friends may call you narcissistic.
* If you identify with 6, then instead of mulching you'd really rather be hanging out in a Bohemian coffeehouse drinking espresso and quoting poetry to arty friends.
* If you see yourself as 7, then you have a pretty unusual social life when you're not in the garden.
* If 8 is your mulch of choice, you'll never have trouble getting your kids to help with gardening chores. Nor will you have to go around begging folks to take surplus produce like most gardeners do—not only will they flock to your garden, they'll weed it in gratitude.
* You admit to 9? Don't go away. I have a fantastic used car for you. Don't need a car? How about an oil well . . . or the Brooklyn Bridge?

What to Do When Bugs Bug You

One of the biggest challenges facing any gardener is the never-ending war with insects. Talk to a gardener and you're bound to hear ten times more talk about cutworm, screw worm, coddling moth, gypsy moth, Japanese beetle, squash beetle, potato beetle, Dutch elm beetle, grasshoppers, scale, and thrip than you'll hear talk about begonias, petunias, chrysanthemums, geraniums, or daffodils. But regardless of the kind of plants under your protection, the following tips should help you cope with the creepy crawly critters that feast upon them:

* If you have a musical bent, consider composing a symphony

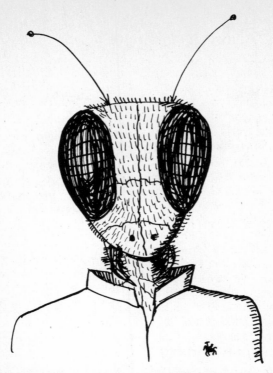

from that wonderful cadence of chirping, clicking, buzzing, and rasping of wings. It won't be easy to orchestrate, but if you can coax the little guys to cooperate, the end result will be well worth the effort. And you'll have no problem getting the players to show up for rehearsal.

* Tone-deaf gardeners needn't feel left out. Almost every species of insect can be trained to march in step, and will not object if the music of the drum and bugle corps is canned. Add some teeny-tiny uniforms with brass buttons, spats, and epaulets, and your pals will really look classy marching along the stalks and leaves in perfect cadence.

* Ever notice how green aphids congregate on green plants, white ones on the paler flowers, yellow spiders on yellow petals, and so forth? Lucky for us, many insects have a fantastic color sense and flock to the plants with the most flattering hues. Shrewd gardeners use the insect's instinctive good taste to their own advantage. Select loud, clashing color schemes for your garden and no fashion-conscious bug would be caught dead near it.

* Keep in mind that garden insects are cold-blooded and

generally vicious. Even "beneficial" bugs are voracious killers ("beneficial" is not the same as "benign," after all). So look to the world of international power politics with its opportunities for scheming and double-crosses. Just a bit of innuendo here, a whispered rumor there, and you can manipulate the insect factions into attacking one another. Before long their ranks will be decimated, while you keep your hands clean. Maybe the Pentagon can even justify the neutron bomb finally: instead of killing people while leaving buildings intact, it can zap the bugs and leave the plants still standing.

* Of course, many gardeners *like* personal involvement in aggressive insect warfare, or we wouldn't have such a thriving garden chemical industry. If you, however, have neither the taste for intrigue nor the stomach for violence, you won't be forced to settle for coexistence—not, at least, if you have any kids around. Very young children will capture unwanted bugs with great enthusiasm if you pay them a penny apiece. (If your predators are very numerous, offer to pay by the pound instead.)

* If law enforcement can train dogs for drug sniffing, why not train *your* dog to be a bug sniffer? Surely a caterpillar lurking under one thin little leaf is easier to uncover than cocaine packed into the wrist band of a Rolex.

* To make them more visible to hungry birds, spray the bugs with fluorescent paint. If that doesn't work, sprinkle bread crumbs on their backs to make them more tempting.

* Dabbing cheap after-shave on your flowers to disguise their natural identity is often effective. But if that doesn't work, a thin coat of plastic gloss will do the trick by making them look fake.

* For keeping destructive moths away from the garden, nothing beats fear as a tactic: open your window, turn the volume up as far as it will go on the stereo, and blast forth the death aria from *Madama Butterfly*.

* Swear the old geezer across the street to secrecy and confide that you heard from a very reliable source that (fill in the name of whatever insect especially plagues your garden) is an aphrodisiac, and that you're worried that they'll get stolen at night because you sleep so soundly.

* Hey, so what if the little guys want a piece of the action? Come on, you can afford to be a little generous! Plant a couple of extra rows and mark it down to the cost of doing business,

like the "protection money" shopkeepers in mob-controlled cities have to pay.

* Actually, you don't really need to hassle with insect control at all. Tell your friends that the CIA got wind of your incredible gardening skills and has asked you to take on a special, vitally important assignment. This project also gives you a watertight excuse for not sharing your flowers and veggies when you'd rather keep them to yourself, since everything you grow is now classified top secret.

* Value insects for the positive image they help create. When granola-type guests dine at your table, you can serve frazzled, bug-bitten produce as clear evidence that your garden is organic and chemical-free.

* When all else fails, keep in mind that insects are very nutritious. They're totally natural, organically grown, high in protein—and absolutely free.

Invasion of the Plantbody Snatchers

Most gardeners spend a lot of time whining about wildlife robbing the fruits of their labor. Savvy gardeners don't have to. They know what to do. How savvy are you? To find out, match the animals with the correct course of action in the following column, then score yourself below:

To foil:
1. deer
2. raccoon
3. rabbits
4. birds
5. woodchucks, gophers, and moles

You:
(a) Fasten miniature cowbells to the tops of the stalks to jingle and scare away would-be diners.
(b) Chew up sticks of non-sugarless spearmint gum until they start to get sticky, then glom them to the predator's would-be victims. The gum will lure the culprit away from its original snack (your plant) as a short-term benefit, and in the long run, tooth decay will put the predator out of commission.
(c) Don't chase the hungry animals away. Instead, advertise your garden as a petting zoo and charge admission.
(d) Populate the animal's burrows with trolls and hobbits and the disgruntled creatures will soon give up and move elsewhere.
(e) Put yourself in an affectionate mood, and pucker up. Because

no matter how extreme the measures you take, you can get ready to kiss your garden crop good-bye.

Key: 1-c; 2-e; 3-b; 4-a; 5-d.

How did you do?

If you answered fewer than two correctly, you really ought to think seriously about signing up at your local community college for a course on animal behavior.

Two to three correct answers means you're not as dumb as you think you are but you've still got a way to go.

If you got four correct answers, you're a producer for a documentary series like *Nova*.

All five answers correct makes you either a cheater or a syndicated garden writer. If it's the latter, don't think you can get away with stealing my tips for your own column, because this book is copyrighted.

CHAPTER 5

Trickle-Down Economics

What Every Gardener Should Own

To anyone pondering the merits of starting a first-time garden, the commitment gardening seems to demand is nothing short of awesome: all those shovels, hoes, cultivators, fertilizers, tomato cages, bean poles, vine climbing mesh, seed inoculant—it's like shopping for a wedding gown and monogrammed sheets and his-and-her towels and even a baby layette before you've even gone on the blind date.

So to save you from going on a wild spending spree, we've classified your garden "musts" as either "high-tech" or "high-tone" to go with your lifestyle and temperament. And in case the paraphernalia in neither of these categories quite appeals to you, the author's personal choices are also offered for your consideration.

Seed

High-Tech: Scientists in Cornell University's Department of Plant Genetics recombined DNA from thousands of dissimilar cultivars to develop this series of annuals. Flowers from this seed are drought-, wilt-, mildew-, and smut-resistant. Each individual seed comes with its own 180-day life insurance policy.

High-Tone: Even the exchange rate on the U.S. dollar couldn't deter us from importing this irresistible and elegant European flower seed. Unlike your typical perennials, which give the same old repeat performance year after year, plants from these seeds not only continue to provide a dazzling display for years to come, but also change their entire appearance and blooming style seasonally.

Author's Choice: What a shame to waste those seeds piled up in the back of the garage that you never got around to planting last year.

Fertilizer

High-Tech: One liter of this accurately calibrated formulation will suffice for 100 kilograms of living plant matter. It provides the entire spectrum of essential nutrients and trace minerals in a distilled, ionized base.

High-Tone: An infusion of de-Exxonated Atlantic sea organisms with emulsified Arctic kelp and fillet of salmon will keep your plants mellow. For those special species, add a chaser of our finest horticultural cognac.

Author's Choice: The garden seems like a convenient spot to dump the used kitty litter.

Plant Supports

High-Tech: The most ambitious gardener striving for prize tomatoes can count on the reliability of these vanadium alloy plant cages, which support 900 times their own weight. Those gardening in cramped conditions will appreciate the "Ultimate Space" model, whose self-generated magnetic field causes plant limbs to contract into compact clusters.

High-Tone: Meticulously crafted in a small village near Versailles, according to age-old, patient, traditional French peasant methods, these cherry wood trellises with three hand-rubbed coats of lacquer will give years of enduring pleasure.

Author's Choice: The favorite plants are propped up by a cast-off movie theater display of *No Mercy*, depicting a disheveled Kim Basinger swooning in the arms of Richard Gere. Lesser plants have to settle for the support of sawed-off mop handles.

Plant Ties

High-Tech: Mylar-coated plant ties deflect the sun's ultraviolet rays toward the center of the plant while protecting the stems and leaves from enzyme and hormonal distress upon contact.

High-Tone: Woven from natural fibers, then tinted in soft earth tones, these plant ties are guaranteed to blend in with the palette of your garden, whatever its theme.

Author's Choice: Strips cut from old panty hose.

Watering Aids

High-Tech: The sensors in these electronic irrigators trigger the valve whenever they detect soil humidity has dipped to the lower end of its optimal moisture range.

High-Tone: Hand-cast bronze quail faucets have the gentle patina displayed by only the costliest of genuine antiques.

Author's Choice: Sure, I know all those gallon plastic milk jugs lined up between the rows may make my garden look like a junkyard, but they do the job and they really cut down on trips to the recycling center.

Pruning Tools

High-Tech: Laser cutting implements trim unwanted foliage with ultimate precision while at the same time cauterizing cut edges to prevent invasive organisms from gaining entrance.

High-Tone: We've unlocked the secrets of the ancient Norsemen to provide these pruning shears with the keen slicing edge of a Viking sword. Work best when doused with aquavit.

Author's Choice: Gee, it's such a nuisance to run all the way back for the pruning shears. Most of the time you can just bite off the offending sprig.

Storage

High-Tech: These ingeniously designed storage shelves provide protective enclosure for your entire collection of fiber-optic micro tools, yet telescope into a space no larger than a cigarette carton.

High-Tone: This redwood potting bench is designed to be placed between your converted stone barn and the Victorian-era gazebo built by your great-grandfather's groundskeeper. Serious upscale gardeners will agree that it provides the ideal environment to display burnished antique tools within convenient reach.

Author's Choice: Storage? What's that? Doesn't *everybody* just leave their tools lying out in the garden?

Timekeepers and Data Signaling Devices

High-Tech: DigiGro provides a digital readout not only of time and ambient temperature, but also of humidity, soil temperature, atmospheric air purity, and lunar phase-solar flare synchronicity.

High-Tone: Each passing moment casts its shadow on this stately Italian sundial bordered with patterns gleaned from ancient Etruscan ruins.

Author's Choice: You can tell it's getting late when your neighbor starts hollering at her kid to come in for piano practice.

Education

High-Tech: Don't set foot in the garden without first viewing a comprehensive horticultural video. For more interactive advice, hook your modem up to a garden user's electronic bulletin board.

High-Tone: Just as no dinner table is complete without a Waterford crystal bowl of roses, one's coffee table is simply naked without the latest copies of *Horticulture, National Gardening,* and *Fine Gardening* magazines.

Author's Choice: Why struggle to figure it out? Isn't that what mothers-in-law are for?

The Gardener's Shopping List

When the new garden catalogs come, do they leave you feeling your garden is a Blue Light Special, outclassed in a world where everyone else has Pierre Cardin creations? Or that you're poking along with implements barely a step up from the bone hoes of ancient Sumeria, while those around you zip through their chores with Space Age gadgetry?

After browsing through the seductive enticements in today's lavish garden catalogs, you'd have to be made of stone *not* to get those feelings. Keep in mind that the average catalog editor is a former cult leader with a Ph.D. in mind control. HER SOLE MISSION IN LIFE IS TO GET YOU TO BUY EVERYTHING!

In the columns that follow is a shopping list of the basic "necessities" commonly recommended in garden catalogs. If their lure is so great that you cannot be without them, then don't miss the Appendix at the end of this chapter. If, on the other hand, you're determined to resist the dream merchants' attempts at brainwashing before you get cleaned out, consider the tested and proven alternatives from real-life gardeners, instead.

Garden "Musts" and Garden "Musts" Translated

* Tiered compost sieves, $9.95 each: Bent window screen with a duct-tape-mended rip

* Two pounds of Bio Activator for fast composting, $13.50: Contents of the bottom of the bird cage

* Inflatable owl to keep birds off your berries, $14.50: Handy vocabulary of curse words

* Flanged compost stirrer, $14.95: Old ski pole

* Steel-manganese long-handled trowel, $15.90: Slotted soup ladle

* Goatskin gardening gloves, $17.50 per pair: Two left hands from frayed pairs of cotton work gloves, one worn backward to fit right hand

* Compost thermometer, $18.95: If your compost isn't on the liquid side, use your finger

* Computer for testing pH level of soil, $19.90: Home pregnancy test kit you ended up not needing

* Underwater flower-stem cutter, $21.50: Spouse's new fly-tying scissors or best sewing shears

* Battery-operated $30\times$ power pocket microscope to inspect insects munching your garden, $23.80: Patience to wait till they're fat enough to be seen with the naked eye

* Rolling seeder, $27.95: The human hand

* Danish tool-carrying tote, $34.90: Hideous purse from Aunt Minnie that looks like a funeral urn

* Sturdy teak-stained mountain-crafted magnolia wood trellis, $59.95: If you're well-endowed, old bras stapled to the wall to support cantaloupe

* Two-gallon galvanized watering can with premeasured fertilizer dispenser in pouring spout, $65: Grandma's rusting old enamel coffee pot

* Tinkling brass Javanese wind chimes, $90: The human voice, crooning an assortment from Frankie Blue-Eyes' selection of old standards

* Compost tumbler, $99.95: The patience to nag until someone else gets out there with a pitchfork and turns it

* Cordless grass and hedge trimmer, $159.90: Battery-operated carving knife you never get to

SUPPLY V. DEMAND

use now that all your friends have turned vegetarian

* Terra cotta birdbath with fluted column base, $179: Frisbee

* Ornamental lattice English cottage-style rose trellis: $199.50: For householders: loose front porch siding; for apartment dwellers: fire escape

* Electric power sprayer, $325: Profound sense of resignation and extra free time

* Enameled wrought-iron Victorian garden bench with morning glory vines entwined with fern fronds, $795: Rock

* Hand-cast Durastone replica of fountain in Tivoli (supplies soothing sounds of flowing water), $1,488.50: Hose with cracked washer, permitting continuous dribble

* Interior version of above for indoor garden to achieve inner peace, $1,595: Leaky toilet valve providing background sound of tinkling, trickling, burbling

Loan Application,
Flora Bunda National Bank

Name   Social Security Number   Date of Birth

Address

I have lived at the above address for (how long)_____

Rent__

Own__

Outstanding Mortgage Yes__   No__

Name and Address of Mortgage Lender

Place of Employment

Type of Employment

I have been employed at the above for (how long)

Income_____

Please list three credit references below:

_____
_____
_____

Loan Purpose:

Amount Requested:
Terms Requested:

I state the above information is correct and I hereby authorize
this Bank to investigate my credit and employment history.

Signature_____

Date_____

CHAPTER 6

Gardening as Therapy

In these therapy-oriented days, people are always being urged to express themselves, to avoid bottling up their emotions. Not surprisingly, gardening is one of the activities that therapists urge on the troubled. While I am in the foremost ranks of gardening fans, you should be aware that there are some conditions that even gardening cannot remedy. What follows, then, is a cautionary list of the possible and the impossible.

What Gardening Can and Can't Cure

Gardening . . .

* *Supplies a plausible excuse for compulsive hand washing.* Nobody wants to eat a sandwich made by muddy fingers, or grasp the hand of someone who's just been squashing slugs, so whenever you feel the urge to turn the tap on, you can avoid being pitied as crazy by explaining, to all within earshot, "I've just come in from the garden."

* *Gratifies masochistic tendencies.* What other respectable activity forces you to abase yourself for long periods of time in unnatural positions that cause pain, demands unswerving devotion yet is frequently unprofitable, lowers your confidence, and results in heartache?

* *Satisfies the urge to show off.* Now that public schools satisfy the foreign language requirement with Spanish and Chinese, universities ignore classics in favor of marketing and ethnic studies, and even the Roman Catholic church celebrates

47

Mass in the vernacular, there are fewer and fewer opportunities to be glib in a dead language. What better justification than gardening can you find to let mellifluous phrases like *Grandiflora particularis* trip off your tongue?

* *Indulges power lust.* You don't need play to Rambo to wear camouflage. Even the most externally mild and placid grandmother has a perfect excuse to crush insects, blast weeds, yank up plants by the roots, and fling aside weaker seedlings, without fear of criticism—all with an innocent, angelic smile for observers.

* *Offers justification for social climbing.* In horticulture, it's more than legitimate to give meticulous attention to pedigree. Before welcoming any species into your garden, you'll note that some plants bestow enormous benefits on their companions, whereas others can be next to useless, even harmful. You're allowed to shun plants that breed promiscuously, to avoid those which leave your favorites in their shadow. And no one can call you a snob.

* *Satisfies the craving to be a big industrialist.* When you garden, you can be obsessed with productivity; you can zealously overplant and then find no use for the resulting glut. You may find yourself squandering vast sums on tools you really don't need. You'll toss away plants that have performed reliably for years and replace them with cheaper varieties. Ultimately, everything in your garden except Daikon radishes may get devoured by Japanese beetles—and you get to fight back with your only remaining implement, the John Deere tractor with the Kawasaki engine.

Unfortunately, until scientific knowledge advances a few more notches, gardening can't cure the problems below:

- Sexual frustration
- Baldness
- A dateless New Year's Eve
- A poor report card
- Halitosis
- Acne
- Herpes
- Flatulence
- A bad portfolio
- The common cold

Taboos When Talking with Addicted Gardeners

Most of the folks reading this *Unofficial Gardener's Handbook* are doing so because they are actual gardeners or at least armchair gardeners. However, *some* people may be reading this not out of choice or interest but because they find themselves houseguests in a home with nothing else around to read except, perhaps, *The Encyclopedia of Gardening, A Field Guide to Cultivated Flowers, The Spiritual Essence of Lawn Care,* and *The Zen of Compost.* Do not despair! This book offers something for you, the nongardener, too.

As you no doubt are well aware, spending time with avid gardeners when you are not one yourself can be pretty horrendous. *You* want to talk about disarmament; *they* want to talk about grasshopper infestation. *You* introduce a conversation about cinema vérité; *they* say, "Speaking of films, did you ever see *The Corn Is Green?*" and then launch into a monologue about dates of maturity of different corn varieties—and so forth. To help you avoid triggering a barrage of talk about soil inoculant and the like, we hereby list taboo topics. Steer away from:

* Mentioning the L. L. Bean catalog—or your companion will be reminded of beans.

* Cats. They remind gardeners of catnip, which leads to contemplation of other herbs, so watch out.

* Dogs. Yes, dogs are not a safe subject, either, because the dog days of August are the times folks feel too hot and lazy to garden—but not to talk about it.

* Buying a car. Sure, be a wise consumer and learn to protect yourself by learning about your state's lemon law—but if you mention it to gardening friends, be prepared to hear about citrus growing.

* Revenge. Did you rake a rival over the coals? Keep quiet, or think of another way to boast about it; "rake," after all, is a garden tool.

* Speaking of boasting, if you're

a golfer who just got a hole in one, by no means mention it to a houseplant gardener unless you're ready to hear about drainage holes.

* Business. Indeed, the business deal you're talking about may have a lot at stake, but will you pay the price of listening to talk about plant supports?

* Atmospherics. So your gardening friend is full of hot air, and expects you to believe a bunch of nonsense. If you don't want to appear gullible, then let your lips pull apart with just the faintest suggestion of a grimace, and narrow your eyelids to achieve a squinty, skeptical expression. But *don't* exclaim, "That's just a bunch of B.S.!"— that will open the floodgates for talk about fertilizer.

* Weather. Idle chitchat about the weather has always been the mainstay of small talk in our society. Whenever there's an awkward silence and nobody is sure of common ground, it's always safe to gripe about the heat, the cold, the drought, the rain, the wind. Right? Wrong! Not safe as far as gardeners are concerned. Mention of *any* weather is enough to set them off again, so either keep quiet or prepare to grin and bear it.

* Nature. To be absolutely safe, it's better to avoid talking about *any* natural force, living

thing, or even mineral. This seems really extreme but you just can't be sure. Just try showing off your new diamond engagement ring to a gardening addict, for example. From diamonds, she'll steer the conversation to diamond mining—just to get around to digging in the ground.

Trash Therapy: Good Reasons to Compost

Many gardeners feel a religious zeal when it comes to composting. No matter if their compost pile is nothing more than a heap of rotting garbage: they view its workings as a glorious manifestation of Nature's bounty that keeps the molecules active in the ever-changing cycle of life. If you're not the gushy type, however, consider composting's practical advantages. Composting is like a savings account for your garden: though preparing it is kind of tedious, gradually it piles up and makes richer beds possible.

But composting offers other notable benefits. Just consider, composting:

* Gets rid of pent-up tension. Hurl rotten tomatoes and raw eggs into the compost while thinking about your least favorite person.

* Satisfies your mad scientist urges by allowing you to mix and putter and watch stuff transmute.

* Gives you a moral high, because every time you fling in a leftover olive pit, you can assure yourself that you are helping to save the environment.

* Gives you a chance to get rid of leftovers so you won't have to hear your family complain when you serve them again.

* May save your life. When your four-year-old surprises you with breakfast in bed (which turns out to be a bologna and jelly sandwich), you *may* be able to make a big show of enjoying one bite and then hide it under your pillow until you can sneak it into the compost pile.

* Helps you avoid that terrible sense of guilt when you've pushed all the more complicated food to the back of the fridge because you didn't feel like fussing with it and then it starts to grow mildew; now you can consider it "pre-started" compost.

* Provides a practical use for dog fur at last. This lets you buy a purebred $800 Llasa Apso and still feel frugal. The same holds true for that champion

Himalayan cat that set you back $1,200.

* Allows you, likewise, to pat yourself on the back for frugality when recycling dryer fluff.

* Provides a ready excuse if you're an ax murderer, having an affair, or cheating your business partner. A compost pile is an ideal place to bury bodies, love letters, or invoices.

* Offers privacy. Even if you're just a gentle, trustworthy person with nothing to hide, there are times you long for solitude. Sit down to read, play the guitar, or watch television and the odds are 100 to 1 that somebody in your family is going to interrupt you. But go out to turn a compost pile, and *nobody* will come near you. If they do, just say "Oh, I'm *so* glad you're here—will you please give me a hand turning this pile? My back is starting to ache," and hand over the pitchfork. You can be guaranteed to be left alone there ever after.

CHAPTER 7

Faking It and Making It: How to Make a Good Impression

Excuses Not to Weed

Is your garden weedy? Do people criticize you for sloth and messiness? With the excuses that follow, you'll never appear one-down again:

* Claim it's due to modesty; you hate to show off a meticulously groomed yard and make neighbors jealous.

* Explain that weed roots redistribute deeper soil minerals to the upper level, where deliberately cultivated plants can benefit.

* Tell your friends that weeds act as parasols, providing shade for the more delicate plants.

* Insist that you purposely planted weeds for a "living mulch" to keep more aggressive weeds out.

* Rationalize that those "weeds" pack amazing nutrition, and bore all comers with a monologue about the calcium, beta carotene, and iron content of wild edible plants versus cultivated ones.

* Argue that weeds distract birds, bugs, and rabbits from attacking cultivated crops.

* Tell everyone you're growing them as an ornamental crop; then bolster your claim by sticking jar-filled weed clumps in prominent places around your home.

* Tell them your grandma used to sing you a lullaby about weeds

and now you're too sentimental to pull them.

* Suggest that Shirley MacLaine's alien beings sent those vital growing manifestations as a message of universal peace from a faraway planet.

* Claim they were a gift from your mother-in-law, who'd be insulted if you did away with them.

* Confide that your weeds are part of a vendetta against an unpopular neighbor; not wanting to risk arrest and jail for outright vandalism, you're taking the more passive approach of letting weeds go to seed and blow into his yard.

* Swear them to secrecy and whisper that the weed is really hallucinogenic:

* Pretend weeds have amazing powers to erase wrinkles/cure headaches/increase libido/improve memory, and you may even be able to sell them some.

Grooming and Attire: How to Look Great in the Garden

When you work in your garden, do you feel you're dressed all wrong because you never look anything like the "official" gardeners that appear in magazines and garden catalogs?

The publishers of really upscale garden literature love to illustrate their pages with pictures of frail, aristocratic, silver-haired ladies in pastel print dresses and beribboned straw hats, their flawlessly manicured hands holding armloads of delphiniums in a hand-woven beechwood lug. The earthier publications, on the other hand, prefer for their model a hearty, bearded man showing rippling muscles through the casually rolled-up sleeves of a Pendleton shirt; he's smiling at a young woman who clearly loves weeding his vegetables and living with a man almost as old as her parents. Naturally, if they showed a sweaty person with disheveled hair, looking really grungy, wearing something you or I are likely to be wearing, like a grimy cast-off high school tracksuit, much of the appeal would be lost.

Though we scoff at the exaggerated pretensions of the gardening catalogs and horticultural magazines, let's admit it: most of us secretly would *love* the secret for looking svelte, cool, elegant, and sexy while we're crouching in the dirt trying to dig a borer out of a squash vine.

The following tips may not guarantee you'll look as if you just stepped out of the pages of *Town and Country*, but they'll help you

at least reach minimum standards of grooming, so if you have to dash out to the garden center to pick up a little more fertilizer, you won't have to worry about getting picked up by the police and booked for vagrancy.

Fingernails

Dirty fingernails are the bane of every gardener, and no amount of scrubbing, soap-under-the-fingernails, protective lotion, or industrial-strength cleaners seems to help.

Women and transvestites who cannot tolerate wearing gloves can always hide the grime under dark nail polish or fake fingernails. This solution is not acceptable for straight men. However, it *is* considered okay to go around with grimy nails if you're a member of a skilled craft or trade. No one would dream of criticizing a cabinetmaker if his nails were dark from wood stain, would they? So even if you work on Wall Street, when your nails won't come clean, wear heavy-duty work shirts with your name embroidered on the pocket, and if you're lucky, you'll be mistaken for a mechanic.

Shoes

Have you noticed how the models in garden magazine illustrations are generally shot from the knees up so we don't see what they're wearing on their feet? If the feet *do* show, they're likely to be fashionably shod in color-coordinated clogs or immaculate Wellington boots, not because *real* gardeners look so fancy, but because their publishers are hoping to sell ads to the manufacturers of those products.

In true life, unfortunately, we *are* visible from the knees down, and (if we're wearing any shoes at all) are more often clumping around in a pair of increasingly multilayered shoes that nobody would pay to advertise. The layers are old, hard, dried mud superimposed with wet, sticky, new mud. And, depending upon the tilth of your soil and the degree of wear on your soles, the clumps might be studded with lots of little stones.

When all these layers start to weigh you down, leave your shoes out on a rainy day or kick them off under the sprinkler. At the very least, the water will wash away the outer mud layers. If you're *really* lucky, though, your shoes will disintegrate or a neighbor's dog will run off with them, and you'll get to buy new ones.

Sandals

Whatever you do, beware of those $1.19 made-in-China rubber thong sandals, even though they *are* cheap, comfortable, and washable. They create suction and glue you to the mud—something which can be not only aggravating, but possibly fatal. This author was imprisoned between rows of lettuce that way when a deer came down from the woods and attacked her in the garden. Pinioned to the mud by her discount-store footwear, she couldn't escape before she was badly battered, requiring stitches and rabies shots, which meant she was too sore to wear jeans and had an excuse to buy two new dresses, which, come to think of it, gave her the best-dressed garden season, ever.

Feet

Many folks prefer gardening barefoot. If you don't step in manure or on a rusty nail, this is often the most comfortable way, and of course avoids the problem of muddy shoes. The trade-off, though, is muddy feet. If you're in business or the professions and you're male, muddy feet are actually an advantage, because dirt blends so well with the conservative, yukky colors well-dressed men are expected to wear. It may even be possible to give the illusion you're wearing shoes and socks without bothering to don them.

If you're a woman and you have no time to wash your feet after gardening barefoot, wear dark panty hose. (No matter how much you disapprove of gender stereotyping, if you're a woman you won't be able to get away with the fake footwear, and if you're a guy, don't try the panty hose. Sure it's unfair, but that's life.)

Stomachs

Mud doesn't only create problems for *feet*, however. Sooner or later you're bound to find yourself reaching down to move the hose when you're all dressed up to go somewhere. The next thing you know, you've got muddy hose prints snaking across your stomach.

Short of gardening naked, the best solution to this problem is to choose brown clothing, preferably with a busy pattern. For executives in pin-striped suits, however, this is not possible. Executives are therefore best off leaving their gardening chores to hired service.

Headgear

Beginning gardeners sometimes think that hats are only a fashion affectation, but that isn't true. As they used to say in the heyday of the British Empire, "Only mad dogs and Englishmen go out in the noonday sun." So unless you are one of the above, it's vital that you select protective headgear.

You needn't settle for the hillbilly look by sporting a traditional red-peaked cap with a FUNK'S HYBRID insignia, or a battered wide-brimmed straw hat that looks as if it belongs on a mule, though. Pick a hat that reflects your true personality, such as baseball caps of winning teams, camouflage-gear combat helmets, Dr. Livingstone-style safari hats, captain's yachting hats, or expensive handmade pioneer sunbonnets from mountain craft fairs.

Warning: You may have seen some really hokey hats for people in various pursuits, such as hats with wings sticking out for runners, ones with moose heads mounted on top for hunters, beer cans for partyers, and so forth. But if you want to convey even a shred of dignity or class, resist the impulse to wear a hat topped with a zucchini, or even a flowerpot.

When All Else Fails

Is it possible to ignore all fashion advice, be as sloppy as you choose, and still look debonair? Maybe. If you can't pull it off successfully and you *do* meet criticism for bad grooming and terrible attire, though, you have some recourse. Claim you're in the process of designing a scarecrow and are trying to find out which image scares the birds away most successfully.

Correct Couture: What the Well-Dressed Garden Should Wear

Even if by nature you're not an especially envious person, there's nothing that's likely to leave you feeling worse than reading garden literature. Of course, many gardeners eager to improve their gardening skills do turn to gardening books, catalogs, and magazines for guidance, but it would be a terrible mistake to take all the extravagant claims and chichi photographs seriously.

No editor between California and Maine would ever feature a land-scape cluttered with weeds, piles of dog do-do, forgotten suntan lotion bottles, and a broken lawn mower, although common sense tells us that many of us have yards that really look like that at least some of the time. And the magazines never show harvests piled into disintegrating cardboard boxes leaning against a broken screen door—instead, they're piled into pyramids in copper bowls on the butcher-block counter of the earth-tone kitchen with its built-in atrium, cunningly adorned with kumquats and avocado leaves.

Fortunately, help is at hand for honest folks who will never achieve the gardens of flawless perfection, but want to pretend they can: Paper Doll Garden Accessories and the concept of "Garden Dressing." The concept of "Garden Dressing" lets you compete with even the snootiest garden perfectionists. Even if you live in a backwater like Onalaska, Wisconsin, there's no need to fret. Thanks to our "Garden Easy" plant paper doll wardrobe, your garden can hold its own against the servant-staffed elegant grounds of the finest English manor houses.

With our "Garden Easy" plant paper doll wardrobe, a mere flick of your wrist achieves what it takes other gardeners months, even years, to accomplish. The small sum of $34.95 (including postage and handling) brings you this amazingly realistic, meticulously crafted, durable plant wardrobe.

Once you try it, you'll discover a multitude of practical advantages. Following are just a sampling of the many versatile benefits you'll enjoy year after year:

* *Corn Coveralls* disguise your cornstalks, fooling raccoons into thinking your tender, ripe Illini Super Sweet are really just pole beans.

* *Pole Bean Boleros* lull your kids into mistaking that plenitude of green vegetable that's destined for their plates for a row of sunflowers.

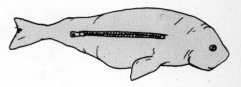

* *Zucchini Zippers* swiftly enclose each and every zucchini in your garden with fuzzy, adorable pelts resembling endangered species. Keeps your much-loathed harvest under wraps and well protected until the exact moment you are ready to foist it off on unsuspecting neighbors and friends.

* *Sunflower Sweaters* relieve that skinny shapeless look, flesh out the contours of the gaunt stalks, and add a touch of blush to sallow flowers, transforming them into veritable American Beauties.

* *Petal Frills* add a touch of graceful elegance to any vegetable. Even a drab little cabbage undergoes a metamorphosis when softly draped in this lush, richly textured designer item. Available in choice of Spring, Summer, and Autumn palate. Winter hues not available.

* *Brooks Brothers Broccoli* gives frivolous flowers a more buttoned-

down look. Projects an aura of nutritious seriousness to even the most flippant flora.

* *Weed Cloaks* shield your domain from the eyes of critical neighbors, while allowing you to avoid the backbreaking labor of uprooting intruders. The ecologist's answer to toxic herbicides, these charming, fashionable, multicolored weedwear items have the added advantage of discouraging plant conception.

* *Rock Hats* save you the labor of hauling off heavy stones from your garden. Simply top them off with a selection of jaunty headgear, and you'll be the envy of everyone around you. Choose from the following assortment: (a) peaked caps with equipment-manufacturing emblems, team emblems, or beer brands; (b) wide-brimmed, black felt, waterproof Stetsons; (c) jogger's eyeshades; (d) yachting captains' models; (f) sequined, plumed pillboxes with wisps of netting à la 1940s movies.

* *Balcony Begonias*, unlike traditional plant paper dolls, are heavily weighted to prevent toppling by heavy wind, and so are ideal for apartment dwellers coping with the challenges of balcony gardening. Simply plunk these over empty pots (the ones that previously contained live plants).

* *Dandelion Disclaimers.* Do your friends tease you for being a perfectionist? Do envious neighbors resent your success in achieving a flawless lawn? Then blunt their criticisms with these realistic and rapidly removable dandelions, which can be speedily whisked away again when you're entertaining folks with better taste.

* *Lawn Blankets.* Turn your lawn into a velvet paradise that would be the envy of any golf course owner with our breathable, heavyweight Lawn Blanket. No need to mow, as this compresses even the most unruly underlying vegetation. Its textured, vivid-green nap resists fading and will last for years. Unlike Astroturf, however, our lawn blankets interact in a most wholesome manner with the ecosystem, permitting weeds and insects to flourish naturally.

Lawn Ornaments

Some misguided people think that a garden consists merely of some rosebushes or cabbages springing forth from the soil. Not so! Any serious-minded gardener should know that a garden is also "a statement." First of all, it displays your tastes and judgment for all the world to see. No less important, it also reveals a great deal about your social status.

For these reasons, prudent gardeners know that lawn ornaments are every bit as integral as tomato cages and bean poles to the well-planned garden.

But before rushing out to buy some geegaw to decorate your lawn, it's important to consider the message your lawn ornaments proclaim. Are you trying to fit in? Cast a landed-gentry aura? Prove you're "just plain folks"?

The following guidelines rate lawn ornaments from highest to lowest class to help you select those that best reflect the *true you* (or at any rate, the desired *false you*).

1. Huge, rusting, indefinable hunks of welded steel commissioned from a sculptor at a cost of thousands of dollars.

2. Classical Greek marble statuary of a naked cherub pissing in a fountain. This is acceptable only if belonging to an archaeologist or classical scholar from an Ivy League school. Be forewarned that otherwise people will consider you pretentious and will snicker behind your back. They'll also suspect you of either getting rooked as a gullible tourist and having a fake foisted off on you or trading in illegal antiquities and dealing with grave robbers.

3. Authentic terra cotta wall sundial from medieval Britain.

4. Replicas of terra cotta medieval British sundials. Unlike Num-

62 *Shelley Goldbloom*

ber 2 above, if this item is in your possession, you will be suspected of nothing worse than being middle class. Since these replicas are generally purchased through very pricey catalogs, you'll at least be considered upper middle class.

5. Cast-concrete grapevine-entwined birdbaths in the style of the Italian Renaissance, but manufactured in Minnesota.

6. Cow-mingos—like the pink flamingos that flutter in the wind, but painted with black and white spots like cows, denoting that the owner possesses a sense of satirical irony—a true sign of an intellectual person.

7. Wild geese that flutter in the wind. These are designed on the same principle as the pink flamingos, but are preferred by less frivolous folk espousing environmental causes.

8. A whole flock of pink flamingos.

9. Mercury balls. You'll never see these ornamenting the lawn of the more elite, who are afraid of appearing common but secretly lust for them because they are beautiful and mysterious and look like giant Christmas tree ornaments and reflect the sky and trees in a magical way, while making your own reflection look funny.

10. A plaster statuette of the Virgin Mary ensconced in an altar of an upended bathtub adorned with shards of blue glass from broken milk of magnesia bottles.

11. Glass gallon jugs filled with colored water radiating in a circle from the top of a pole.

12. An iris growing from the center of a truck tire slashed into serrated triangles resembling the teeth of a jack-o-lantern.

13. A galvanized water tank sliced lengthwise and planted with tulips.

14. Painted plywood cutouts of a fat lady's fanny surrounded by painted plywood dwarves and toadstools with polka dots.

15. Geraniums ensconced in a seatless porcelain toilet bowl.

16. 1,679 corncobs glued together into a spitting likeness of Elvis.

17. Huge rusting hunks of welded steel up on blocks, originally commissioned from a Detroit automaker at a cost of thousands of dollars.

Score yourself:

(a) If you answered yes to item number 1, your name is really Baxter Haverford III and you ought to pass this book on to the executive director of your landscaping staff.

(b) If you answered yes to two or more of the items numbered 2–5, then you ought to drop your membership to your garden club and send dues instead to the Friends of the Metropolitan Museum Of Art.

(c) If you answered yes to any of numbers 6–10, your garden must have an enormous number of plant varieties, your garden implement collection is the envy of every other gardener in your neighborhood, and your VISA Gold Card is your favorite gardening tool because you love to shop.

(d) If you answered yes to at least one of numbers 11–16, you no doubt plant your petunias in elaborate alternating color schemes all down the rows. Even though you had to take metalwork in high school and so didn't get to take art, you have a very creative spirit. You might want to consider plotting your entire garden on graph paper and converting it to a paint-by-numbers wallhanging.

(e) If you admitted number 17 applies to you, then you are either the eccentric scion of an old, moneyed family named Baxter Haverford IV, or your name is Duane and you barely have time to garden because the demolition derby is about to start in half an hour and you have to stop off first and pick up some more chewing tobacco.

CHAPTER 8

The Spiritual Side of Gardening

Gardening as a Religious Ritual

Committed tillers of the soil believe the garden bed is as close to heaven as anyone can get without actually dying. The really spiritual sowers and reapers know, though, that it's possible to establish even closer celestial ties through the intercession of a patron saint.

Just as many drivers safeguard themselves with a plastic dashboard statue of Saint Christopher, patron saint of travelers, gardeners desiring special protection can erect little garden effigies of the patron saint of gardeners, Saint Horticulturion. Horticulturion was also commonly revered as patron saint of doubtful causes before the advent of Wall O'Water.

The missionary Saint Horticulturion journeyed to the Far East after he had a dream instructing him to go forth and teach the heathen to grow cole slaw vegetables-and potatoes for proper Sunday dinners once they were converted. After battling a horde of potato bugs he succumbed to exhaustion during zucchini harvest and died a martyr's death.

Times That Try the Soul

Every true saint knows a time of testing. You know you're bucking to fill in for Saint Horticulturion when:

* The heat wave that made it agony to work in the garden finally ends—just in time for mosquito season.

* Your wife finds that expensive Danish beer you'd been saving for a special occasion and uses it for slug bait.

* In the middle of the night, on a dare, the kid next door turns

in a false alarm and the fire truck parks right in the middle of your garden.

* The day you're having a fancy dinner party your child lovingly picks you a bouquet of dandelions for the dining table.

* As soon as you finish harvesting one hundred pounds of prize potatoes, your husband announces he's going on a diet and refuses to touch anything except brown rice and grapefruit.

* A sparrow builds a nest in your scarecrow's pocket.

* Cutworm decimate all your pepper and tomato plants but never lays a tooth on the zucchini.

* A zillion cockroaches see your spider plants in the window and, believing they're cousins, move in.

* Your Boston fern gets so homesick in Los Angeles that it dies.

* Your seeds decide to become actors and start rehearsing for the part where the seeds all fell on fallow ground. Mark 4:1–7

Holistic New Age Gardening

New Age gardening synthesizes the wisdom of the ancients with the sophisticated, aware, cutting edge of modern pseudoscience to bring you a garden radiating an energy force that is healthful, calming, harmonious, and synchronized—and much more spiritual than your brother-in-law's garden, even if he *does* grow bigger tomatoes. Following are a sampling of the wondrous mystical avenues that you, as a dedicated holistic gardener, may want to explore:

Meditation

Some schools of meditators, such as the Transcendental Meditation folks, practice deep meditation by means of chanting a mantra. If the mantra is in proper synchrony with one's deepest essence, it will generate a state of profound concentration in the chanter.

Possibly one of the following mantras will resonate with your soul state. *Warning:* You're never supposed to reveal your mantra, so *don't tell!*

BUR-PEE
CUL-TI-VAR
HY-BRID-IZE
HY-DRO-PON-IC
PHLOX

However, if, like Thoreau, you opt for the simple American form of transcendentalism to fill you with harmony, then forget about chanting. To go into a trance, simply bend over to pull a weed, and before you know it, you'll discover that you've been puttering happily, unaware that hours have gone by.

Crystals

Old-time gardeners claimed you got better crops of peppers and tomatoes by strewing a handful of Epsom salts at their base. Soil scientists guess the magnesium salts give a boost to plant metabolism. Proponents of the New Age lifestyle, however, know better: the special power pulsing deep within the laxative crystals is what keeps things moving.

You can also tap into the power of the crystal through gravel mulches. Although often sneeringly dismissed outside of tract-home landscaping, white quartz shrubbery mulches actually help the roots communicate with the cosmic forces surging throughout the universe.

Soil Chiropractic

Do you have sandy soil? In the dark era before New Age, people believed that scratching in manure and decomposed vegetation improved soil drainage. Enlightened folk recognize the *real purpose* is to free the sand particles so that they may transmit and receive untrammeled harmonic vibrations.

Clairvoyance

In ancient times, oracles used to predict the future by examining the organs of goats and chickens. In our own era, when so many people are adherents of vegetarianism, and the Humane Society and shrink-wrap packaging act as deterrents, you may be glad to know that animal guts aren't necessary for reading signs and portents. It's also possible to read the future in the entrails of vegetables. Here's how:

With a sharp steel knife in the dark of the moon (so your neighbors can't watch and report you), pierce the heart of an artichoke. (If you don't live in California you may not grow artichokes, but then,

if you don't live in California, why would you be doing this anyway?) You can, if necessary, substitute a punctured cabbage.

Recite the first poem you were forced to memorize in eighth-grade English and think profound thoughts about eternity. Reach deeply within the chosen vegetable and remove its frailest inner leaves. With all your strength, fling these high into the air. Scrutinize the pattern they form upon landing.

If you did this right the leaf pattern will reveal the following:

* The best mutual funds to buy into

* How many pounds you'll lose on your new diet

* Whether you should splurge on that stereo you've been eyeing

* Which set of in-laws you should eat with *this* Thanksgiving

* The winning combination of next Saturday's lottery

Numerology

Many New Age gardeners are rediscovering the mystical belief system from the ancient cabala called numerology. Numerology assigns a number to each letter of the alphabet. Combinations are either lucky or unlucky. For example, with A being 1, B being 2, and so forth through Z-26, we discover that the numbers in the letters WHEELBARROW are terribly unlucky and best avoided.

Totalling the dangerous number 130, this open one-wheeled vehicle possesses dangerous magic qualities that, merely by filling the barrow with newly harvested onions and leaving them overnight, call forth fierce downpours. Its scoop (represented by an ominous 68) shape ensures the onions will lie in a pool of water and go mushy before you get back to them.

Soul Music: Bach or Rock?

Plants respond to music just as we do. After studies showing plants did better with a diet of Bach than with the Rolling Stones came out, many gardeners were afraid to listen to anything but highbrow music in the vicinity of their gardens. But if sopranos accompanied by harpsichords are not to your liking, don't despair.

"It's sheer intellectual arrogance to assume that plants prefer baroque to rock," states a spokesperson for the American Society of Horticultural Musicology. "Unfortunately, plants, like humans, are all too often fooled by outward appearances. So groups with names like the Rolling Stones and Farm Accident scare them. But just look how they thrive on Nitty Gritty Dirt Band."

Plant Bonding

Thanks to the interconnection of all living things, plants not only like you to talk to them, but can read minds, sense human emotion, and distinguish friend from foe. This explains why plants in office environments easily droop and die.

The begonia on the windowsill may indeed be able to judge the sincerity of your lover's intentions. But why trust the course of your romance to a plant so moody? To play it safe, watch the zucchini.

Astrology

Moon-phase gardening would be simple if you only had to notice the shape of the moon as it waxes and wanes. But the proper time to plant seeds, transplant, cultivate, prune, harvest—or to can, brew, and pickle—ties into the moon's monthly path across the night sky relative to the constellations of the zodiac.

Every two or three days the moon is influenced by another of the twelve signs. Some signs are feminine and fertile. Others are masculine and barren—the kiss of death for plants and people unlucky enough to be planted under them.

As guides to garden astrology, many gardeners rely upon almanacs. Unfortunately, rival almanacs often offer contradictory advice. For instance, one tells you to plant potatoes under Capricorn and onions under Aries. Another prefers Taurus and Sagittarius for these plantings. Smart New Age gardeners schedule their garden tasks under the calendar signs of "A Day with No Dentist Appointment, Aerobics Classes, or Car Pooling."

CHAPTER 9

The Secret Life
of Plants

Passion in the
Garden Bed

Shelley Goldbloom
Rural Route 1
Onalaska, WI 54650

Dear Shelley:

I have received your manuscript for our *Unofficial Gardener's
Handbook* and frankly, I'm disappointed. You agreed to write a
book covering ALL essential aspects of gardening. Our readers
deserve nothing less. Please recall that in our preliminary discus-
sions pertaining to this project, you led me to believe that it
would include a detailed explanation and thorough counsel on
PLANT SEX.

And yet upon numerous occasions when I attempted to pin you
down regarding the contents of this chapter and date of delivery,
you became evasive and switched the subject. As the deadline fast
approaches to complete the final editing of this manuscript, not
a single paragraph on PLANT SEX has crossed my desk. Ante up!

Yours truly,

Alexia Dorszynski

Alexia Dorszynski, Senior Editor

To: Alexia Dorszynski, Senior Editor
NAL/Dutton Division of Penguin USA
375 Hudson Street
New York, NY 10014-3657

Dear Alexia:
   It's really upsetting when you complain I've been evasive, pro-
crastinating and failing to fulfill my contract obligation. You hotshot editors sit there in fancy offices with one measly Boston fern
drooping on top of a file cabinet—what do you know about real
gardening, anyway?
   Let me tell you, I've been a gardener for twenty-eight years
and neither myself nor any of the other real gardeners I know
have the slightest desire to think about passion in the garden
bed.
   Certainly our plants breed, but so did our mothers, and *they*
didn't talk about it, did they? Well, plants are like parents: they
can go about their business cross-pollinating or whatever it is that
they do, in private, without making a big fuss to *us* about it.
   Frankly, I think your generation has sex on the brain because
you grew up with The Pill, Lenny Bruce, Woodstock, string biki-
nis, those filthy Jordache jeans ads, and *Cosmo* magazine.
   Well, there are still plenty of people from my generation alive
(despite what you might wish) who grew up with a proper respect
for discretion and propriety.
   Back in our day, there wasn't any such thing as "Sex Educa-
tion" in the school curriculum. (Even my biology teacher never
went beyond clams because she didn't want us to get ideas. And
when she went around the room making kids take turns reading
from the text, you'd sit there cringing because there were "dirty
words" like *pistils* and *stamens* and *ovaries* coming up in the
middle of the chapter and you'd just know by the time they got
to those paragraphs it'd be *your* turn and you'd die of embar-
rassment if you had to actually say them out loud.)
   So trust me: as far as the potential market of older readers are
concerned, leave out all that filthy stuff because it's just one step
away from pornography.
                                        Sincerely,

                                        Shelley Goldbloom

                                        Shelley Goldbloom

Shelley Goldbloom
Rural Route 1
Onalaska, WI 54650

Dear Ms. Goldbloom:
 I must insist that you comply without delay! If you do not, my publisher has instructed me to return your manuscript and demand remission of all advance moneys paid.

Yours Truly,

Alexia Dorszynski

Alexia Dorszynski, Senior Editor

To: Alexia Dorszynski, Senior Editor
NAL/Dutton Division of Penguin USA
375 Hudson Street
New York, NY 10014-3657

Ms. Dorszynski:
 (a) You nag me to write about "hybridizing." Well, the idea of group sex disgusts me, and I am morally opposed to orgies.
 (b) There is enough steamy raw sexuality in the media without a good, clean garden book making a big to-do about "pheremones."
 (c) With Gay Liberation constantly being thrown in our faces and grown men hugging and kissing in public we've no need to have "asexual reproduction" adding insult to injury.
 (d) Maybe *you* can be blasé about depraved "relationships between plants and pollinating insects" because you're so used to seeing those high-priced prostitutes in New York City strutting around walking poodles on leashes as a sexy come-on, but polite people don't want to think about it.
 (e) As to plant birth control methods like corn detasseling and using plastic bags to protect plants from sexual contact—can you honestly say you're not just looking for an excuse to fling "vasectomies" and "condoms" in readers' faces?
 (f) Maybe they really *are*, as you say, transferring hormones into plant genes to make them resistant to insects, but as far as

I'm concerned, this kind of folderol is akin to having silicone breast implants—it's unnatural!

(g) Finally, you wanted me to say something about how, thanks to the wonders of horticultural genetic research, plants don't have to "do it" the ordinary, natural way anymore and can have test-tube babies, like humans with all that sperm bank and surrogate parent nonsense.

Okay, you're going to give me an argument about the younger generation of readers, to whom you no doubt cater because they're so extravagant and would think nothing of throwing down $7.95 for a book they could just as well borrow from the library. Well, most of them are too busy climbing the career ladder to even cook a dinner from scratch or phone their mothers, let alone fiddle with plant propagation.

So take my advice: leave sex out of a good, clean, interesting garden book like this and save that smut for Gothic romance novels, okay?

Yours Indignantly,

Shelley Goldbloom

Shelley Goldbloom,
Discriminating Author and
Real Gardener

From: Alexia Dorszynski, Senior Editor
To: Legal Department
Please draft letter to Author #55820-472 terminating contract.

Thanks,

Alexia

Alexia

Where the Wild Things Grow

As people go, many gardeners are a conservative lot, minding their own business and hoping to avoid interference by government or nosy neighbors. Sometimes plants have other ideas, however, as you can see by the following documents:

ARREST REPORT

WESTCHESTER COUNTY POLICE DEPARTMENT CASE #7836226

NAME	ALIASES
Zea Mays Rugosa	Seneca 60, Iochief, Country Gentleman Illini Supersweet

OFFENSES
Disorderly Conduct
Vagrancy
Sexual Assault-2nd Degree
Resisting Arrest

ADDRESS
Migrant

HOME PHONE	PLACE OF EMPLOYMENT
None	99 Fern Acres, Scarsdale, NY 7th row corn patch

ETH. ORIGIN
Mixed (Hispanic, Yankee, Indian)
DATE OF BIRTH
8-15-91

HEIGHT	COMPLEXION HAIR
6 ft. 3 inches	golden tan dark, silky

DISTINGUISHING PHYSICAL CHARACTERISTICS

One ear markedly larger than the other.
Listed subject was approached by police officer in response to a complaint from subject's next-door neighbor. Said neighbor had expressed alarm that subject was attempting to cross-pollinate her

corn. Moments before her complaint was received, said neighbor alleges she had discovered her immature corn in a state of great agitation, corn silk in disarray and flailing about with pistils exposed.

Subject refused to cooperate with arresting officer or admit his stamens had emitted pollen into the neighbor's yard. He muttered that he had lost control of his stamens during a high wind and was not cognizant of the alleged pollen discharge.

Due to the large crowd of onlookers (believed to be relatives of the purported victim), officer took subject into custody for his own protection. When informed that he was under arrest and read his rights, subject refused to come willingly, requiring officer to use firm persuasion. Without undue force, officer grasped subject behind the ears and exerted sufficient pressure to push him into a horizontal position on the ground. During the scuffle, subject flung dirt into officer's hair and eyes.

Subject was handcuffed and had to be forcibly restrained in the back of the police vehicle for the officer's safety. However, subject refused to remain upright and sprawled across the backseat, spewing yet more dirt as he did so. During the ride to the police station, subject swore a continuous stream of what appeared from the loud and abusive tone to be obscenities, but in a language not known to the police officer.

At the police station, subject claimed he had been unable to respond when questioned by officer because he suffered from corn earworm injuries sustained in childhood. Subject complains of his stalk being sore from being kneed during the scuffle ensuing from his arrest. He was booked on the above charges, transported to county jail, and incarcerated until he makes bail.

COUNTY OF WESTCHESTER
CIRCUIT COURT BRANCH #2
OFFICE OF PROBATION AND PAROLE
DATE 10-30-92
PRE SENTENCE INVESTIGATION

Since his arraignment nearly three months ago, Defendant Zea Mays Rugosa has become shriveled, lost significant weight, and seems to be in poor health. It is evident that the weeks of incarceration and the stress of the trial and conviction have taken its toll on this formerly insolent, cocksure cornstalk.

The juvenile case worker in the District Attorney's office states that a difficult home life, lack of proper supervision, and a great deal of peer pressure all contributed to the defendant's situation.

Defendant is the offspring of Central American peasant stock, accustomed to a milder climate and noncompetitive environment populated with compatible species, who survived by eking out an existence any way they could on impoverished, sandy soil. Finding himself transplanted to the affluent environment of Westchester County, the defendant felt out of his element. How could he gain acceptance among the elite hothouse hybrids with sophisticated pedigrees that were now his companions?

Nor could he turn to his parents for guidance because the INS (Immigration and Naturalization Service) had denied their plea for asylum, claiming they were economic, not political refugees, as they alleged.

The fact that this young cornstalk flaunted his virility at a far too early age also was not his own doing. For centuries, the Rugosa family had been content to follow their ancient, primitive folk traditions, maturing at a measured pace after the August full-moon ceremony, then mating and bearing offspring according to the time-honored schedule of their progenitors. But now, Machiavellian experiments conducted secretly in genetic-engineering laboratories have created unnatural hormonal changes calculated to thrust the youth into premature maturity.

Surging through his plant cells were juices and urges he couldn't understand and couldn't control. From an ancestry with 93-day maturity, the helpless Zea now was plunged into full maturity after only 68 days with no time to gain experience, or learn wisdom.

The court may also wish to take into consideration the lack of appropriate role models in the defendant's life, for over countless generations not a single member of the Mays Rugosa tribe has ever had exposure to a consenting form of pollination.

Due to the above circumstances this office recommends the court employ compassion when sentencing the above defendant.

DISPOSITION
Defendent was sentenced to three years in state prison. Sentence was stayed and defendant was released under his employer's supervision with three years' probation. As a condition of probation, Defendant is ordered to undergo counseling.
11/15/92

The Social Complexities of Companion Planting

Every gardener knows that when planting the perfect garden, attention must be paid to the position given each plant—some horticultural specimens are just like the kid who brings home a report card that says he "refuses to work or play well with the other children." If the gardener is not to have a revolt in the garden bed, attention must be paid to the predilections of its occupants. And even then, you can get into trouble . . .

April 15th

My Dear Leticia,

Please forgive the delay in replying to your letter, but words fail me when I try to describe the incredible emotional strain that I have been under. Preparing a seating chart for our forthcoming gala planting season is proving difficult beyond my wildest imaginings.

I sent invitations to every garden dweller on your list, and, with few exceptions (Cilantro, Beet, and Ground Cherry), all responded in the affirmative. Now I am struggling to arrange compatible companions, taking into account their quirks, peccadillos, grudges, and suspicions based upon year after year of those tedious old (and seemingly never-to-be-forgotten) relationships.

Who would have predicted, my dear, that ordinary garden-variety plants would prove so temperamental? One is led to the conclusion that many of these so-called companions would benefit from the expertise of a gardener far less than that of an analyst, especially the following:

Cucumber (So paranoid!)

Tomato (You'd think the garden were a high school, with all those cliques.)

Potatoes (My dear, I never dreamed he was hated by so many!)

Eggplant (He always seemed thick-skinned, but is really quite dependent.)

Radish (Being assertive is one thing, but she's so *aggressive!*)

Cauliflower (Was she *always* this spiteful and catty?)

Dill (A born victim if there ever was one.)

Bean (Codependency is more of a problem here than any of us suspected.)

Sunflower (Despite that tall, strong, cheerful facade, he's terribly vulnerable.)

Originally, I'd planned upon seating Tomato in the center of the row, because despite her faults, she *is* interesting—but it is becoming impossible to put almost anyone near her!

I'm thinking it's a wise decision to place Tomato near Mint, for whom she has developed quite a "thing," claiming her health and flavor are at their best in Mint's company. And Tomato and Carrot are good friends. But who else is acceptable? I cannot place her near Cauliflower, because it's common knowledge there is bad chemistry between them. I've also been warned to keep Kohlrabi, Cabbage, and Potato at a safe distance because none of them get along well with Tomato, either.

Potato, I figured, could go on the other side of Cucumber, Pumpkin, and Squash. Thank heavens you reminded me how they continue to brood about poor Potato lowering their resistance to blight, and avoid his company. And Sunflower is persona non grata with Potato, rumor has it, for stunting his growth on numerous occasions.

I hoped I could make at least some headway seating Cucumber far from Potato near some of the Aromatic Herbs who have enough character not to be overwhelmed—you know how she tends to take over, given half a chance. It had completely slipped my mind that the Aromatic Herbs and Cucumber have only gotten along together outside the garden bed.

I suppose I can put Cucumber next to Corn, which should please old big ears, providing him with some protection from that dreary Wilt-causing Virus. While I'm at it, maybe I can squeeze in Bean, who's rumored to be pretty compatible, if you know what I mean. Just seeing the way Cucumber takes every opportunity possible to wrap around his stalk shows you there's something funny going on there.

(Tell me, by the way, does Dill belong to the Aromatic Herb family? They all are kind of peculiar, and take some getting used to. And what is so horrible about Dill that Carrot has such a dislike to him?)

And I'm reminded (for the umpteenth time) that Eggplant also wants to be near Bean, seeking protection from Colorado Potato Beetle's threatened takeover.

Let's see, that still leaves Radish, who, I suppose, could go by

Cucumber, who's such a wimp about those Beetles when forced to cope alone.

Mon Dieu! This gives me a headache. I wish planting season were over!

Yours Most Affectionately,

Blanche

Blanche

Lust for Land

Sometimes what starts as passion for the soil, for a nice little garden patch with a good amount of sunlit tilth, becomes an overweening, unstoppable lust for land. Real estate salesmen know this, and are forever strewing the gardener's straight and narrow with temptations that threaten to bankrupt and cozen him. And the situation is worsening. Just consider, this, which arrived yesterday.

Plantation Estates: Invitation to a Modern Eden

Are you a discerning organic plant, willing to settle for nothing less than utmost quality in every phase of your life?

Do you dream of putting down roots in the pristine earth of a quaint, historic former colonial ant settlement?

Can you picture yourself prospering in an elegant natural environment, undefiled by cheap soil additives and mass-produced herbicides?

Whether you are a corporate field crop with vast space requirements, or an individualist opting for solo container dwelling, our executive garden development may well be the answer to your dreams.

We are pleased to announce that Phase I of Plantation Estates is now offering select homesites to the qualified buyer. Both panoramic-view outdoor row sites and protected interior condominium windowsill locations are available.

At Plantation Estates, never will your right to privacy and exclusivity feel threatened by aggressive crowds of inferior, chemically grown species. For in order to qualify, every buyer must submit proof of impeccable organic authenticity to stringent scrutiny from our selection committee.

In this green paradise, you won't be disturbed by the hubbub of mechanical cultivators. Our tilth is maintained by a flock of purebread earthworms under the supervision of a certified organic greenskeeper.

And you'll be free to leaf out to your heart's content, watered by our own private spring-fed reservoir, which supplies an unobtrusive, underground timer-operated trickle-irrigation system.

For at Plantation Estates, we've spared no effort to provide you with every convenience of modern life without sacrificing the luxury and quiet comfort of the bygone pre-Green Revolution era.

At Plantation Estates, from tender beginnings to harvest years, your life cycle will be suffused with the grace and charm of our unhurried atmosphere.

At Plantation Estates, you will flourish secure in the knowledge that you belong to one of horticultural society's most prime biotic segments.

Harmony and beauty await you at Plantation Estates, the Garden World's elite, exclusive Eden. To learn more, call 1-800-555-1176.

CHAPTER 10
Harvest Glut

As every gardener knows, the first fear is that nothing you've planted—not even the rare and exotic Trumpet Daffodil bulbs, at six dollars each—will come up in the spring, and you'll be humiliated before your mother-in-law and the members of the local gardening club. As spring turns to summer, however, that first fear passes, only to be replaced by a second, deadlier fear: you planted all those tomatoes (zucchini, snap beans, cauliflower, INSERT YOUR BIGGEST MISTAKE HERE), and now someone's got to take charge of the little buggers, which are threatening to take over your backyard and cannot be handled by the canning room in the basement. Yes, fellow gardener, it must be faced: you have garden glut, and you'll need all of your ingenuity to deal with it.

"There's got to be more Potatoes down there! Keep digging!!"

Shelley's Laws

✳ First Law of the Garden:
The productivity of any crop will be in direct proportion to your family's dislike of it.

✳ Second Law of the Garden: The friendliest people are always those with vegetables to unload from their own gardens.

✳ Third Law of the Garden: Non-gardening acquaintances, who might have been expected to pick up the slack, invariably have vegetable allergies or are out of town on vacation.

The Zucchini Problem

It's a sad fact of life that nobody respects a pushover. Any garden crop that's finicky to grow and keeps you guessing about the outcome wins adulation and status, but a plant that puts out for virtually everybody without any coax-

ing will be despised as a round-heeled wanton regardless of its beauty, generous nature, and easygoing personality.

Even if *you*, though, truly do champion zucchini as a splendid vegetable, and feel nothing but sincere gratitude for its bounty, you soon enough find yourself stymied to know what to do with so *much* of it. Inevitably, sooner or later the big challenge will be divesting yourself of the surplus.

This is no easy matter, because by the time *you* have zucchini to dispose of, so does everybody else, and the competition can get pretty tough. Keep in mind that getting folks to accept zucchini is a lot like getting them to lend you money: you should never just ask them outright. The job takes shrewdness, nerve, and finesse. The following strategies will help ensure success:

* Stuff neighbors' mailboxes with zucchini while they're asleep. Choose moonless nights; remember, stealth is the key.

* Save plastic grocery sacks, the lightweight kind with two-hole handle grips. They're strong enough to hold several small or one huge zucchini and are ideal for hooking on doorknobs, permitting a quick getaway.

* Volunteer to go door to door for the March of Dimes, Heart Fund, and every other summertime charity campaign. It provides a great opportunity to expand your zucchini route. You have a legitimate excuse for ringing doorbells—along with asking for money you can offer people squash. If they're not home, see the preceding suggestions.

* Politically minded gardeners might prefer this variation: offer to campaign for a political candidate. Choose someone who faces a late-summer primary election that coincides with your zucchini crop. If you pick a candidate facing close competition, you may even be lucky enough to get a second go-round with an election runoff. And if your candidate loses, you can pelt the winner's motorcade with rotten squash.

* Have lots of dinner parties early in the garden season so you'll amass lots of return invitations by the time the zucchinis appear. If you opt to bring zucchini instead of flowers or candy, your host is still obligated to accept your gift graciously.

* When proffering zucchini to anyone, realize that an unadorned zucchini is merely a common vegetable. So save pretty containers, gift wrap, and ribbons. Friends would be churlish to refuse a beautifully decorated package. You might even be able to disguise a bow-

topped, tissue-wrapped zucchini as a bottle of wine.

* Recipes with imaginative uses for zucchini abound. Take advantage of them, and then don't be shy in sharing the results. But don't be too pushy. Remember: Marie Antoinette lost her head when she insisted, "Let them eat cake!"

* Human beings are not the only potential recipients for surplus zucchini. Using zucchini instead of a ball or newspaper, teach your dog how to catch. Offer to teach all your neighbors' dogs as well. Note: Do *not* teach them to retrieve.

Five Ways to Recycle a Melon Rind

1. Cut open your melons when they're too green to eat. They're never going to ripen now, so assuage your conscience over the waste by tossing them onto your compost pile.
2. Wait until the melon is overripe before cutting it open. Unfortunately, you can't serve a melon that's squishy and fermenting; once again, the compost pile is the answer.
3. Never quite get around to eating the melons you left sitting on

your kitchen counter; when you notice fruit flies milling around and soft spots tinged with bluish mold, toss those babies into the compost pile. If you feel too guilty watching them rot, put the melons in the refrigerator toward the very back of a shelf, hidden behind a loaf of bread and a half-gallon of milk. Then you can legitimately forget about them until they're sufficiently transmuted.

4. Plan a huge party and invite everyone you know. Cut up lots of melons into little cubes to spear with maraschino cherries on toothpicks. Then lure your guests with prawns dipped in cocktail sauce, sweet-and-sour chicken wings, paté, and rumaki. When everybody goes home, remove the toothpicks from all the uneaten fruit kabobs, eat the cherries, and toss the melon into the compost pile. (P.S. While you're at it, dump the leftover dribbles of booze diluted with the melted ice into the compost, too. The compost bacteria get a quick though short-lived kick. And they can't grouse if they ever get hangovers!)

5. Rummage through all your recipe files until you locate Grandma's recipe for pickled melon rind. Run up and down the basement steps four times hauling up boxes of old mason jars. Dust off the cobwebs. Wash the jars with soap and

water, after shaking out the dead flies. Rinse them well (the jars, not the flies). Make a special trip to the store to buy new rings and lids so the jars will seal properly. Shave the peel off the watermelon rind, then meticulously trim the rind into evenly sized little squares. Measure out the sugar, cinnamon sticks, cloves, and other expensive ingredients according to direction. While the syrup is simmering, wipe up spilled sugar from the counter. Sweep sugar granules up from the floor. Remove your shoes and take them to the bathroom sink to swish the stuck sugar granules from the soles. Sterilize your mason jars. Fill them with syrup and pickled melon. Carefully seal. Gently place the filled jars into a canning kettle. While waiting for the water to return to a boil, wipe the dribbled syrup off the counter and floor. Throw the half-dozen towels needed to wipe up the spills in the washing machine. Return to check on the jars in time to watch them burst. Listen to the tinkle of shattered glass swirling in the boiling water bath. Watch limp pieces of pickled melon rind float to the top of the canning kettle. Capture the pieces. Debate whether it's worth taking a chance on someone dying from ground glass mixed in the pickled melon rind. Reluctantly decide it maybe isn't, and dump the whole soggy mess of melon into the compost pile.

Shortcuts for Coleslaw Lovers

Coping with the Core Ingredients

Although people love to make snide cracks about zucchini and tomato glut (even this book is full of them), the truth is, *those* crops actually are fairly easy to cope with because they mature just a few at a time over weeks.

With cabbage, on the other hand, you're likely to produce two hundred and twenty pounds of mature cabbage from a mere three pony packs of spindly seedlings—and in just a few weeks.

All that coleslaw is a daunting prospect. What should you do with it?

Traditional Method for Heirs Store the cabbage in the cool root cellar that's available because your great-grandfather dug it when he first farmed the land four generations before you inherited.

Conventional Method for Optimists Trundle the beautiful big green heads downstairs to your basement and store them between the power tools and ski equipment. About two weeks later, breathe carefully through your mouth so the stench won't penetrate your nostrils as you haul two hundred and twenty pounds of slimy, mold-covered cabbage out to the compost heap.

Alternate Methods for Realists
• Establish an orphanage.
• Throw a family reunion.
• Move to Iowa.

Adding a Dash of Color

Although folks who fancy themselves gourmets mix pineapple, beets, and all kinds of other nonsense into their coleslaw, traditionalists know that no shredded cabbage worth its salt would call itself coleslaw comingled with anything but *carrots*. With the techniques below you can opt for self-sufficiency and bypass the plastic-wrapped, unnaturally clean, supermarket carrots which non-gardeners are forced to buy.

Labor-free Method Leave carrot crop in the soil and dig fresh year-round as needed. When carrots are desired, crouch in mud, wobbling and wriggling each entrenched carrot from its earthen grip. Become impatient and plunge a digging tool alongside. Listen helplessly to the snap as the root breaks off, then lift out the truncated stump.

Problem-free Method You can avoid the preceding problems by storing carrots between layers of sand. If you live in Hawaii or Florida, finding clean "wild" sand should be a simple business (just be sure to sift out cigarette butts and used condoms).

Gardeners located in northerly climes can purchase sand from a building supply dealer (estimate two sacks @ $2.50–$3.50 each plus $1.50 worth of gas). You may be tempted to snitch "free" sand from the highway department piles kept in readiness for strewing on icy roads. Be forewarned this may be mixed with salt, and eventually your carrots will shrivel, a punishment that serves you right.

Once you've secured the sand, go to an appliance store and wheedle them out of a large cardboard carton. If they won't accommodate you, detour to K Mart and buy a twenty-gallon plastic garbage pail (about $9.95). Carefully embed each layer of carrots in layers of sand. Separate the carrot/sand layers with layers of newspaper and sheets of clean new plastic, which you should be able to find if you look under the old paint rollers down in the basement.

Then insulate the entire exterior with scraps of carpet held together with masking tape and old twine. If you do not have scraps of carpeting that you shoved into a closet years ago in the knowledge that "someday they'd come in handy," then phone around to carpet installers and cajole one of them into saving you some. Top the whole thing off with more newspaper, wadded together and wrapped in garbage bags.

Whenever you need a few carrots, all you have to do is dash into the garage, squeezing past the front bumper of the car, fling aside the layers of carpeting, plastic, and newspapers, rummage in the sand, bring the carrots indoors, and scrub away the embedded grit under running water. (Sweep the sand off the floor.)

Eventually the remaining carrots will start to shrivel or grow whiskers. These are wonderful for amusing bored children, who can be convinced that such manifestations are alien beings bringing urgent messages to our planet.

Sooner or later, a cold snap will freeze your remaining carrots despite all your careful precautions. Then you can haul the whole kit and caboodle (except the plastic pail—if you used one—and carpet scraps and plastic sheeting, which you'll want to save for next year) out to the compost heap.

CHAPTER 11

Murphy's Laws of Gardening

Murphy's Law was named for the philosophical fellow who explained to humanity why it is that bread always falls buttered side down. The universal principle, according to Murphy, is: "If anything can possibly go wrong, it will—and at the worst possible time."

Though Murphy's origins are cloaked in obscurity, there is little doubt that he received his inspiration in the garden, for in no other field of endeavor does his pessimistic law more apply. Abandon hope that any skill or foresight on your part can prevent this,

because Murphy's Laws of Gardening, like the Law of Gravity, put you in the grip of circumstances totally beyond your control.

Following are a few examples, with space for you to add some of your own.

As Ye Sow, So Shall Ye Weep

* The finer the seeds and the more impossible to handle, the more likely they are to dump out of the package all at once.
* The more impossible the spilled seeds are to retrieve, the rarer they were and the farther away you had to send for them. Corollary: You'll never drop the dime-a-package ones. (Console yourself, though, it could be worse—unlike Onan, when you spill your seed upon the ground you won't be punished.)
* Once you've sowed your seeds and carefully marked them by impaling their respective empty seed packets on stakes at the end of each row, the first wind will blow all the paper packets away and your signposts will disappear. Not only will you have lost the location of your rows, you won't be able to recognize any of the seedlings when they appear because the descriptions are gone. And, of

course, your instructions for thinning and care have also vanished. Corollary: If by some stroke of fortune the wind does *not* blow the seed packets away, rain will dissolve the print, leaving it illegible.

* When the preceding mishap doesn't occur, you will pull up your new crops, mistaking them for weeds. If you try to avoid this by marking the rows with twine, a dog is bound to appear and run away with it.
* Whichever corner of your flower bed you earmark this year for your very special favorites will be the same spot where last year's Jack-o-lantern seeds got tossed. They'll sprout incredibly aggressive vines, go on a rampage, and eventually smother everything in their vicinity.
* If you go to the extra trouble of selecting drought-resistant plant varieties, you can count on a wet year.

When You Bet on Father Time, Jack Frost Wins the Photo Finish

* When you have enough self-control to postpone planting

your tomatoes and peppers until the proper time, the spring will have record high temperatures. Corollary: If you plant early, the thermometer will plunge below freezing that very night.

* There's always frost the night *before* you harvest tomatoes.

* Anytime you get ready to mulch your roses by digging heaps of dirt and hauling it all to a protected place and covering the piles so they won't freeze—all in order to have it ready to spread after the ground gets good and hard— an early snowstorm will beat you to it. Corollary: If you rush the season, it'll rain and all the dirt you mounded around the rosebushes will dissolve into muddy puddles.

Tramping Through the Vineyard Where the Grapes of Wrath Are Stored

* The apartment balcony you so lovingly turned into a bower is an inviting natural oasis not only to you but to a pregnant pigeon.

* Just when the pelargoniums on your windowsill are starting to flourish, a construction crew starts to remodel the roof and soot and debris come blowing down.

* Wherever you kneel to dig a new planting hole will be the spot a cat has just chosen to use as a litter box.

* When your peach, plum, or grapefruit tree is laden with ripe fruit, birds will always peck one little hole in every single piece, like kids biting into every chocolate to see what's inside, and then sneaking the rejects hole-side-down back in the box. And the birds are shameless—they leave the holes in plain view. Corollary: On your apple trees you'll never find more than one wormhole per apple, but you can count on it—the biggest and best-looking apples will be the ones to host the worms.

* While you're paging through your recipe files trying to decide whether to make cherry pie or cherry cobbler or cherry wine with your bumper crop of cherries, a flock of raider birds will descend on the tree and devour the entire crop.

* Raccoons always strike the night *before* you're planning to harvest your corn.

Beating Your Ploughshares into Swords

* The tool you need right now is always the one your neighbor has borrowed.

* When you weed and your hoe snags on the stem of a plant and snaps it off, it's never the flower you didn't much care for or the feeble tomato plant you were thinking about culling anyway; you can count on it being a specimen that was your pride and joy—or the cutting that came from your mother-in-law's prized rosebush.

* Whenever you water, your hose executes a deathblow, and like its fellow weapon, the hoe, always goes for the best and the brightest.

* You're out of washers whenever you need to irrigate, and the hose connection leaks, causing water to spurt into your face with great force. But by the time it reaches the nozzle the stream lacks the power to muster more than a feeble trickle.

* It always rains right after you water. Corollary: It always rains the morning you'd scheduled to mow the lawn.

* The lawn mower is always out of gas when you're in the mood to use it. If your grass is *really* long, especially if you're rushing to mow because you're leaving town for a two-week vacation, then the mower isn't just out of gas, it's out of order.

* The day your flowers finally burst into glorious bloom your neighbor's child will appear without permission to pick her mom a bouquet and not only take every flower in bloom, but will pull the plants up by the roots.

Add your own examples of Murphy's Laws here.

1. _____
2. _____
3. _____
4. _____
5. _____
6. _____
7. _____
8. _____
9. _____
10. _____
11. _____
12. _____
13. _____
14. _____
15. _____
16. _____
17. _____
18. _____
19. _____
20. _____
21. _____
22. _____
23. _____
24. _____
25. _____

CHAPTER 12

Gardening Through the Ages

With a history going back to Adam and Eve, you can just bet that gardening has seen great days. Here are just a few of the more memorable moments of the noble profession: Great Moments in Gardening History

BEFORE

AFTER

✱ 776 B.C. Garlic is designated the original "Breakfast of Champions" for its purported strengthening qualities and is included in the Olympic team training diet. Greek sprinters win all the races until their competitors get wise and demand breath testing.

* 218 A.D. Hannibal leads his army across the Alps. The trail of dung left by his elephants on the barren mountain soil helps the rare edelweiss to gain a toehold in the ecosystem and inspire flower lovers for millennia to come, including Heidi and the Von Trapp Family Singers.

* June 2, 455 A.D. Hordes of Vandals sack Rome, inaugurating the word *vandalism* by burning garden tools, cutting down rosebushes, kicking cabbages, and smashing flowerpots.

* 886 A.D. The death of Basil I, founder of the Macedonian dynasty, leads to a brief period of unrest while various herbal factions grapple for ascendancy. Briefly, Cilantro holds sway. But betrayed by the treacherous Oregano, he's vanquished by Leo the Wise.

* Circa 1060. Lady Godiva makes her famous tax protest, putting an end to her husband Leofric's threat to levy a tax surcharge for each bushel of onions harvested by his downtrodden peasants. The greedy earl agrees to squelch the tax after Godiva rides naked on horseback through the streets of Coventry pleading, "Read my hips."

* October 31, 1517. Martin Luther nails his 95 Theses to the door of the Castle Church at Witten-berg, launching the Protestant Reformation. The impassioned theologian neglects to return the hammer to his gardener, who can't repair the trellis, as a consequence of which all the rosebushes fall down—which is why you'll see roses in Roman Catholic paintings, but rarely in Protestant art.

* 1620. Contrary to popular belief, most Pilgrim fathers reject Squanto's advice and refuse to plant corn. Asked why he resists nouvelle cuisine in favor of maggot-ridden, moldy English wheat and barley stores, Miles Standish's next-door neighbor replies, "With fortune's blessing, we'll holde out until Wonder Bread."

* 1778. Swedish botanist Karl Linnaeus, creator of our modern plant classification system, dies; his mother and sisters sell his famous plant collection to an Englishman. The king of Sweden deploys a man-of-war to recapture it on the high seas, and fails. The unfortunate king consequently flunks Horticulture, as the hard-nosed professor won't accept the royal excuse, "But I lost my notes."

* October 16, 1793. An outraged French populace beheads Marie Antoinette for retorting, "Let them eat cake!" to the news that her subjects are starving. Little known fact: far from

being flippant, the poor queen was simply offering to sustain the masses with her vast zucchini cake supply.

* 1853. Naturalist James Morrow is aghast when hostile natives boil the seeds he collects on Commodore Perry's expedition to the Orient. "They should have stir-fried them," concurs the gourmet Perry.

* 1880. Paul Cézanne is so busy painting *Fruit Bowl, Glass and Apples* that he has no time to prune and spray his fruit trees and they fail to bear, forcing the artist to use wax fruit as models.

* 1921. Famous American plant breeder Luther Burbank publishes his eight-volume *How Plants Are Trained to Work for Man.* "What better workers could anyone ask for?" reviewers marvel. "There are never hassles about age discrimination and you don't even have to offer benefits."

* 1941. Plants not seen on English soil since the days of Queen Victoria suddenly spring to life all over London. Did German bombs expose long-buried seeds to light and make them germinate? Noted plant psychologist Professor Sigmund Frond scoffs at this common theory. "Some plants are macho and thrive under pressure," argues the professor. "They'd flourish even more dramatically if they were flung from a window of a speeding Orient Express by an evil stranger."

* April 1967. Daylight Savings Time goes into effect. Although daylight is one of the few things left you can save and not get taxed on, serious gardeners lobby for abolishment on the grounds that this unnatural tampering with the clock exposes vulnerable plants to a lethal dose of sunshine.

Plants of the Future

Remember when chartreuse cauliflowers first showed up in the market? It might have seemed logical to conclude that our mania for tinting hair green, poodles pink, and carnations blue had now spilled over into the world of vegetables. But it turns out that the bilious green vegetable dubbed broccoflower isn't artificially dyed, it's a genetic cross between broccoli and cauliflower. Actually, that shouldn't surprise us, with the sophisticated plant research going on nowadays. Here are some more garden wonders we soon can expect to find.

So popular is the tomato with home gardeners that we can foresee tomatoes taking the lead in expanded and improved selections like the six below:

* Soon tomatoes will rival chocolates and wine as the gracious gift to bring when visiting. A basket of your finest spicy *Bloody Mary* tomatoes, with twenty-percent alcohol content and faintly redolent of dill pickle and celery, will delight any host. *Virgin Mary* is an alcohol-free sister variety.

* *Clamato*, a rather fishy-tasting seedless tomato that liquefies the moment it touches a pot and eliminates the need for peeling, pureeing, or straining. Ideal for linguine sauce and seafood soups.

* The *BLT* is a bacon-flavored tomato growing within an edible, leafy green husk developed for vegetarians and people who keep kosher, but especially for the gardener-on-the-go who's accustomed to a fast-food diet. However, release has been delayed due to lack of enthusiasm in the younger test markets, the common objection being, "You still have to make the toast."

* *Career Girl* and *Yuppie Boy* both thrive in sunless apartments and on smoggy balconies. They adapt to exceptionally small enclosures by an acutely sensitive avoidance mechanism that keeps branches and leaves from intra- as well as extra-species contact. Another interesting adaptive feature of both varieties is that the longer they last, the tougher they become.

Tomatoes aren't the only plants with innovative marvels in store for us. On our horizon are a wide array of designer vegetables, herbs, fruit, and even houseplants promising to make life easier and brighten our future:

* *Pampers* is a highly ornamental potted plant that develops an absorbent diaperlike web among its roots, protecting your wallpaper from leakage and destructive dripping when you water.

* *Mother Love* is the ideal hanging houseplant for homes with curious children or plant-snitching houseguests. This fiercely protective spider plant variety bites anyone attempting to pull off its babies.

* Having already developed a garlic that doesn't give you bad breath, the Japanese are now hoping to penetrate the American market by crossing it with a martini olive for a variety named *Powerful Yen*. A domestic version, aimed toward business travelers, is named *Sake to Me*.

* *Chivato* is a chive-flavored baking potato with a shiny, reflective outer skin that eliminates the need for wrapping in aluminum foil.

CHAPTER 13

Gardening for the '90s

Gardens in the Media

Gardeners know how fascinating horticulture is, and that's why they'd rather talk about gardening than virtually any other subject. Unfortunately, unenlightened non-gardening media moguls mistakenly believe that stories about food, decorating, scandal, babies, sex, science, crime, human relationships, and politics are what the public wants. If the media ever comes to its senses, here are leads for far more important garden features that we hope to see:

Bon Appetit

Now, don't get nervous and start ripping up those garden-variety radishes for fear they won't be fancy enough for the palate of real gourmets. It doesn't matter what varieties you plant, because they're all going to taste indistinguishable once we disguise them with fancy sauces anyway.

Interior Design

The fact that you gag on brussels sprouts, haven't the slightest use for sage, and have no desire ever to taste an eggplant doesn't matter; that rich, glossy purple is the "in" color this year, and nothing complements it better than the muted tones of sprout stalk and sage green.

National Enquirer

Lady Di horrified when Martian seed invades Kensington Gardens, growing two-headed, man-eating lettuce.

Baby Talk

Living Dolls in Cabbage Patch!

True Confessions

A Hybridizer Bought Me to Be His Sex Slave.

Omni

Unraveling the cutworm genetic code may someday help us breed whole societies of Mensa members.

Police Detective

Vigilante ladybugs repel voracious gang of stalkers.

Cosmopolitan

When It's Fair to Fight Dirty: A trap with sensual bait in the dark of night melts those macho moonlight predators.

Seventeen

Insecure conformists fear they can't attract slugs unless they follow the crowd and pour beer into saucers. Smart teens know they'll have throngs flocking to lap up Coca-Cola Classic.

New Republic

Are totalitarian ant colonies less of a threat now in Eastern peonies?

Aerobic Gardening

Occasionally you'll run across some garden hotshot who comes forth with a "no work" gardening method.

Ignore them.

Like they say in aerobics class, "No pain, no gain." In fact, one of the major benefits of having a garden is that caring for it *is* strenuous, and so you can count on it to give you a good workout and burn up lots of calories.

Below are a few common exercises, each accompanied by a breakdown of energy expended by a 150-pound adult engaging in the stated activity for one hour.

Naturally, you can knock off fewer calories if you continue for a shorter period or weigh less, but unless you're really good at arithmetic, it's really simpler to stick with calculations used by exercise physiologists and just keep working longer or gain a few extra pounds.

∗ Walking to neighbor's to retrieve the cultivator he borrowed and never returned: 600 calories.

∗ Driving to local nursery and supermarket and K Mart to check out bedding plant prices: 157 calories.

∗ Chasing dog out of your garden: 900 calories.

The Amazing Porta-Garden *

- Perspiration from Brow gently waters leaves
- Steam rising from body gives Plants that Steam Room Effect.

*(multiple layers of sweats required)

---

* Retrieving row-marking twine the dog ran off with: 1,013 calories.

* Trying to remember location of rows before the dog's arrival for refastening twine: 162 calories.

* Chipping manure off the bottom of your gardening boots with your garden journal pencil: 192 calories.

* Washing manure off pencil

before you write in garden journal: 210 calories.

* Shouting curses at the birds that just pecked holes in every tomato: 122 calories.

* Bending to harvest bush beans: 294 calories.

* Standing upright and picking pole beans: 172 calories.

* Picking pole beans if you factor in the following:
Going to basement to get saw: add 612 calories. Sawing old brooms off wooden handles: add 456 calories. Returning saw to cellar: add 612 calories. Borrowing neighbor's posthole digger and pounding broom handles into ground: add 1,631 calories. Digging shattered broom poles out of soil: add 1,400 calories. Rummaging in basement in vain search for suitable scrap lumber: add 850 calories. Driving to home supply store for bamboo bean poles: add 157 calories. Pounding purchased poles into ground: add 1,009 calories. Returning neighbor's posthole digger: add 600 calories.

* Pouring two ounces of beer into saucer to place in garden as slug bait: 96 calories.

* Drinking ten ounces of beer remaining in can (includes sum of calories expended in the act of drinking plus the calories contained in the beer): 214 calories.

Support Groups for Gardeners

When times get tough nowadays, many of us no longer lean on friends or relatives for support. Instead, we have support groups to help us cope. If we want to stop drinking, we attend Alcoholics Anonymous while our kids go to ALANON, and then when they grow up, to Adult Children of Alcoholics. We also have Gamblers Anonymous, Overeaters Anonymous, Shoppers Anonymous, Parents Without Partners, even Mensa, if you want support even though you're a certified genius.

But if you or someone close to you has ever suffered uncontrollable cravings to pinch off dead roses or imprison a fern in a plastic pot, where can you turn? The world of gardening has need of support groups, too. Here are some we'd like to see flourish:

* WAG: Wives of Addictive Gardeners

* HAG: Husbands of Addictive Gardeners

* ACGP: Adult Children of Gardening Parents

* CWBFG: Children Who've Been Forced to Garden

* MAD: Manic and Depressed Gardeners

* KIABTEG: Know-It-All-Better-Than-Everyone Gardeners

* OOGD: Overly Optimistic Gardening Dreamers

* GTGOOW: Gardeners Trying to Get Out of Other Work

* GRP: Gardeners of Reluctant Plants

* PCUG: Plants Co-Dependent Upon Gardeners

The Executive Gardener

Gardening used to be considered a relaxing leisure-time activity. But nowadays folks are so much busier that there hardly *is* any leisure, and you may feel you're just looking for punishment if you struggle to fit garden chores into an already overcrowded timetable.

If this is *your* problem, don't despair. The following advice from leading time-management experts at Fortune 500 companies offers even the most stressed-out gardener the executive secrets for enjoying a glorious garden:

* Efficient managers know how important it is to delegate authority and show trust. Sure, it's hard to sit idly by, wondering if the seeds you sowed are going to prove reliable. But if you jump to conclusions when you don't see results immediately, and replant, you're bound to wind up with two plants for every position.

* You may be able to get away with being a control freak vis-à-vis your kids, or your underlings at work, but in the garden it will be your undoing. Once you plant seed, *do not* get impatient and dig them up to see if they've germinated. If you do, the good news will be that they have sprouted; the bad news will be that your meddling snapped off the sprouts.

* Don't be bamboozled by glowing reputations of certain plants; behind the impressive garden catalog résumé often lurks a goof-off. Take asparagus, for instance: it will take advantage of a soft bed and live high off the land all year, thanks to your benefits, yet produce for only a few days in return. If, on the other hand, you want a crop that works for you, go for something humble like bean sprouts. They'll be perfectly content in a mason jar and produce results almost instantly.

* It's an unfair fact of life that the taller you are, the easier it is to grab success, and this is true not only in the work world, but in the garden, too.

Spreading, large-sized plants know how to occupy more space and elbow out their smaller, less aggressive brothers. So forget about compact, smaller-sized crops, like carrots, even if you prefer them, and plant watermelons.

* By the same token, raise apples instead of raspberries, because it only takes a couple to make up a pound. Also, apples won't squish on your clothes and leave awful stains, so you'll save extra time on the laundry end, too.

* Consolidate flowers and vegetables in the same beds. This lets you cope with both your meals and your floral centerpieces at once, saving the time you used to spend running back and forth between them. To speed things up even more, train your pole beans to climb up the roses, so you can harvest both without moving position, thus achieving maximum ergonomic efficiency. (It's even more labor-intensive to abolish flowers altogether—try the frillier lettuces, for instance, which are almost as pretty as petunias anyway. Furthermore, green has been scientifically proven to generate creativity, while bright fuchsias, lavenders, and purples will make your plants jumpy.)

* Considering the time and labor pulling weeds requires, it's more cost-effective to spray them silver and reassign them to the decorative category.

* Keep all your plants in pots on your desk. That way, when you're trying to make a phone call and they stick you on hold you can squeeze in the time to cultivate them.

* Instead of sowing seeds in garden soil, simply toss them on the floor of your car. The crusts from old peanut butter sandwiches your kids dropped, combined with heat from your car radiator and the greenhouse effect of freeway fumes, provide an ideal growing environment. They'll thrive.

* By switching to silk shrubs, wax fruit, and plastic flowers, you'll save the time it takes to weed, prune, fertilize, water, and cultivate. You will, however, have to dust occasionally.

* The Ultimate Time Saver: a hologram of flowers on a blank cement-block wall.

CHAPTER 14

The Last Word on Gardening

Gardeners as Literary Critics

Once you learn about gardening, expect to become an expert on more than hard-core gardening topics like begonias and beetles— you'll be an authority about all kinds of things, even today's literary fiction.

To prove how easy it is, here is a practice assignment for your scrutiny: an excerpt from the Regency romance *Thorns in the Heart*. It's the tale of two lovers who possess a secret obsession. Our heroine, Cynthia, is the sole living descendant of the ill-fated Van Deusen line. Her lover, Trevor, is the scion of the Bouchard millionaires.

This scene takes place during a weekend fox-hunting house party at the estate of Lord and Lady Throckmorton, within a stone-walled rose garden, the sole remaining portion of the once-grand estate of the proud Plantagenets, who were forced to sell

after the Great War because of mounting taxes. Lurking in the shadows is Trevor's evil twin Adolpho, whom everyone believes has drowned at sea. Adolpho plots to ravish one of the houseguests, Blanche de Coubert, and fling her over the cliff so that Trevor will be accused and go to the gallows, leaving Adolpho in possession of the family inheritance—and of Cynthia.

THORNS IN THE HEART

Trevor and Cynthia have sworn to keep their silent affliction a dark and shameful secret. How could they trust any soul to understand this obsession that held them in bondage so powerfully and relentlessly? For they are—rosarians! As the lovers caress, covering neck and breast and thigh with hot kisses, not for a moment can they forget that they are slaves to an insatiable and even more urgent longing.

"My dearest Cynthia, looking at your Titian tresses, curling in

wet tendrils against my bruised chest, I lose all self-control, I cannot wait another moment—I must thrust it in, deeply, deeply, beloved!"

"No, Trevor—there are many weeks before all danger of killing frost is past. If you plant those Dynasty roses now, you chance all. And if you thrust so deeply, you'll bury their grafts and lose the cultivars. Nothing will grow but dank, evil, riotous tendrils, smothering all that is good and pure."

Trevor gazes into Cynthia's green, almond-shaped eyes tenderly. She can see the affection growing from pulse beat to pulse beat. Gently, his fingers probe, with increasing urgency. Under his skillful touch, silky pink petals part. Bending, his flickering tongue caresses a sepal. Viscous, it glistens, luminous.

"I can't stand it, Trevor!" Cynthia moans. "Look! There are aphids there! Can it be that the Throckmortons' drunken groundskeeper, that sullen lout, has been dilatory? Trevor, Trevor, I know in my heart that you are man enough to satisfy these needs."

Gazing and clasping her heaving bosom in his knotted muscular arms, Trevor replies, "Linger but a moment and I will return to discharge my killing spray with a force so fatal these petals will swoon and ne'er more know need."

Cynthia stretches voluptuously upon a mossy stone wall, the fastenings at the neck of her emerald-green velvet bodice straining against her ripe, firm, full young breasts. Suddenly, from the rows of dank and evil-reeking herbs lurches Trevor's evil twin, the sinister, black-clad Adolpho, who mistakes Cynthia for Blanche de Coubert in the twilight.

Adolpho pauses long enough to snap a long-stemmed rose, still dewed with pearls of moisture from the groundskeeper's recent outburst of attention, from a nearby branch.

With a hard and mocking smile, he fixes Cynthia with a relentless stare and glides closer. The gap between them closes: Cynthia longs to flee, but his stare is mesmerizing and she cannot.

Adolpho holds out the rose. "Come," he commands. "See what I have for you."

Instantly the spell is broken. "You wield no knife—you are not Trevor!" Cynthia cries, backing away. "For never would he sever a rose in such rough fashion, so cells suck air through the firm stalk and it goes limp."

"Furthermore, I'd never remove a rose at a three-leaf juncture instead of a six-leaf one," says Trevor, materializing from the shadows of the endless, centuries-old box-hedge maze. "You're not only a dastard, Adolpho, but awfully dumb."

What is wrong with the story?

(a) Even a drunken, loutish groundskeeper would know better than to water roses late in the day.

(b) Roses should be cut just above a five-leaf juncture, not a six-leaf one.

(c) If it's weeks yet before danger of killing frosts is gone, would roses be in bloom?

(d) If roses are in bloom, shouldn't Cynthia be too hot in velvet?

(e) In any case, shouldn't she know better than to wear velvet while her hair is still wet? It water-spots, you know, especially back in Regency times before synthetic fabrics.

(f) Also, isn't it a cliché for strawberry blondes to wear green? Especially that early in the year, without a tan, our heroine is going to look terribly sallow.

(g) Why was Cynthia such a lazy wimp? *She* should have gone to get the sprayer instead of considering it "a man's job."

If you picked up on *a, b,* and *c,* consider a career as a garden book reviewer—maybe even an editor.

If you guessed *d, e,* and *f* correctly, don't waste time on garden writing when a career in fashion pays so much better.

If *g* was the main point catching your attention, it's surprising you read this kind of trash; you couldn't be one of those hypocrites who spouts feminist rights while secretly having fantasies about swooning in the arms of pirates, could you? For shame!

Inspirational Quotes for Gardeners

If it ain't broke don't fix it.
(Houseplant gardener after spending a fortune on commercial potting mix, spilling old dirt all over the new carpet, and inadvertently injuring the roots while repotting all the houseplants.)

Experience is impossible to come by until you do it wrong the first time.
(Gardener who foolishly planted the tomato plants before May Day and lost them to frost.)

Experience is what you get when you don't get what you want.
(Gardener who eagerly planted the tomato plants before Memorial Day and lost them to frost.)

Why is it we never have time to do it right, but always have time to do it over?
(Author—and maybe Reader.)

They say that time is the best teacher. Unfortunately it kills all of its pupils.
(Gardeners who wisely waited until Flag Day to plant the tomato plants and lost the crop to frost.)

Doctor Root Answers Your Questions

If you're wondering whether you can still write a thank-you note for that wedding gift Aunt Tillie sent three years ago, you can write Miss Manners (on embossed stationary, of course); if your spouse insists on humiliating you by repeating that story about the time you mistook the governor for Billy's coach and caused such a scene, Ann Landers may come to your aid; and Doctor Ruth can give you counsel if the bedroom is your battleground. But where should you turn when your problems stem from the garden bed, rather than the conjugal one?

To Doctor Root, of course! Whether your garden is plagued by Jack Frost or killer bees, big dogs near small bushes, blight, glut, smut, or smog, the wise doctor can advise you. Following are only a few of the many problems Doctor Root has solved for other gardeners just like you:

Dear Doctor Root:
Do plants suck your breath while you're asleep? I never believed in vampires, but my best friend tells me it's the hanging ferns I've got to watch out for.
Signed, Reluctant Bride of Dracula

Dear Reluctant:
Your friend is no doubt referring to that old myth that plants rob you of oxygen at night. Just to be on the safe side, sleep facedown and try not to be a mouth breather.

Dear Doctor Root:
Who are Harry and David? Do you think they'd like to meet us?
Signed, Howard and John in Seattle

Dear Howard and John:
According to my sources, Harry and David are only interested in perfect pears.

Dear Doctor Root:
When my grapefruit tree is heavily laden, the branches get dragged down by the weight and all the fruit get squashed. How can I prevent this?
Signed, Aggravated in Arizona

Dear Aggravated:
Many folks prop up the branches with lumber, but this puts a strain on the limbs and always invites the risk of a heavy two-by-four slipping out from

underneath while you're trying to prop them up, leaving you with a smashed foot. A far safer practice is digging deep holes in the ground all around the tree trunk to give the drooping branches more altitude.

Dear Doctor Root:
    Every time my peas start to sprout, along comes a sparrow and plucks them right out of the ground. Help!
Signed, Dropping My Membership to Audubon

Dear Dropping:
    I advise you to entice a bull snake into your garden. Riveted by the reptilian stare, the bird walks right to its doom in the snake's mouth in a hypnotic trance. Happy shelling!

Dear Doctor Root:
    Recently my wife and I became vegetarians. We no longer permit the flesh of any slaughtered animal to be served in our house, and so it really upsets us that our Venus's flytrap is still carnivorous. What can we do about it?
Signed, Admirer of Albert Schweitzer

Dear Admirer:
    You both are to be commended for your humanitarian views. Explain to your flytrap how you feel about the sanctity of life, and ask it to cooperate. If that doesn't work, try tricking it with morsels of cream cheese molded into the shape of flies. If you *still* don't succeed, console yourself that the flies weren't really "slaughtered animals" because Venus catches them alive.

Dear Doctor Root:
    My mom is real mean. She makes me eat string beans because she says they are good for me but I hate them and I don't think they're good for anything. What do you say?
Signed, Whining Kid in Sacramento

Dear Whining:
    String beans are great for sticking up your nose. This is sure to get you lots of excited attention from your folks who will drop whatever they're doing and rush you to the nearest hospital.
    There the emergency room team will put you on a table in a little room and write about you on a chart just like they do on TV, and like

they just did to the guy who broke his leg in a motorcycle crash and the lady whose pet pit bull attacked her.

Don't try to get away with this if you're older than ten. And it's only good for one try—though you can stick a string bean in your ear another time. Good luck!

Dear Doctor Root:
  People say gardening is good exercise, good therapy, good for your pocketbook and good for the environment, but I'm wondering why *you* do it? Or don't you?
Signed, Curious in Cincinnati

Dear Curious:
  The ultimate purpose of having a garden is to create and maintain an insect oasis.
  And no, I don't. In the first place, I hate insects, so why make life easier for the little buggers? In the second place, I'm stuck in the office answering letters all day, so in my free time I want to go bowling, not hang around in the dirt getting my manicure ruined weeding broccoli.

Growing Alphabet Soup in Your Garden

The late twentieth century is the age of the acronym—everything from LSMFT (Lucky Strike Means Fine Tobacco) to SCUD missiles, from HST to JFK to LBJ, from NIMBY (Not in My Back Yard) to OSHA (Occupational Safety and Health Administration). Now, for those still bewildered by some of the obscure abbreviations in the gardening magazine, we offer a helpful list:

CRAVE: Composters Recycling Assorted Victuals Ecstatically

GLUT: Gardeners Lusting for Unseasonable Tomatoes
ICBM: Incredibly Compulsive Backyard Mowers
IRS: Increasing Reliance on Sunshine
NERD: Necessary Effort Reduced to Drudgery
PLOTS: Palms Lounging on Table Surfaces
POD: Preposterous Ornamental Delphiniums
PRUNED: People Resenting Unappetizing Nauseating Eggplant Dishes

QED: Quagmire of Enclosed Dirt
SOIL: Sensuous Onion-grower Insatiably Luxuriating
USDA: Universally Shady Drainage Area
VSOP: Very Subterranean Old Potatoes

Riding into the Sunset

Congratulations! You've finished this gardening guide* and now you're an expert! You'll know you qualify if you answer "Yes!" to the majority of the situations below:

* Instead of receiving gifts of gold jewelry or expensive cologne, all you ever get are T-shirts or aprons with slogans like "I HAVE A SENSE OF HUMUS."
* The most exciting date on your calendar is your Last Average Frost Date.
* People who corner you at cocktail parties never proposition you or ask your opinion about Pulitzer Prize-winning novels; what they want is your advice on cutworms.
* There's a power failure and you're trapped for five hours in an elevator full of accountants;

*This test is only for those worthy folks who have actually read this guide in its entirety. If you are browsing in a bookstore in a copy you haven't paid for, sorry, the test won't work for you.

you take it as an opportunity to talk about organic gardening.
* When you order a Bloody Mary, you don't care whether the vodka is Smirnoff or Absolut, but you do insist on juice from Better Boy tomatoes.
* When your sweetheart says, "I'm dying to try something different and really exotic," you reply, without missing a beat, "Then how about planting round, burpless cucumbers this year?"
* You're in the middle of complaining to your psychoanalyst about your castrating mother when he interrupts to ask whether you think it's too soon to prune roses.
* When that new chick/guy you're dating gives you a knowing look and asks if you've ever considered giving a whirl to S&M, you retort indignantly, "Certainly not—I've always been perfectly satisfied with Jackson & Perkins."
* You pull the seed pearls off your wedding gown so you can plant them.
* When you finish arranging the geraniums on your apartment balcony and a beautiful white-robed figure appears and announces she's your Guardian Angel who will remain throughout your lease as your divine protectress, you're terribly dismayed because her outstretched wings will cast too much shade.